MW00436207

Apostles

J. I. PACKER

Affirming the
Apostles' Creed

::: CROSSWAY
WHEATON, ILLINOIS

Affirming the Apostles' Creed

Copyright © 2008 by J. I. Packer

This book was formerly part of *Growing in Christ,* copyright © by J. I. Packer, originally published under the title *I Want to Be a Christian.*

Published by Crossway
          1300 Crescent Street
          Wheaton, Illinois 60187

Cover design: Keane Fine

Cover photo: Veer

First printing, 2008

Printed in the United States of America

Unless otherwise indicated, Scripture quotations are taken from the ESV® Bible (*The Holy Bible: English Standard Version®*). Copyright © 2001 by Crossway. Used by permission. All rights reserved.

Scripture quotations indicated as from KJV are taken from *The Holy Bible: King James Version.*

Scripture quotations indicated as from *Phillips* are taken from *The New Testament in Modern English,* translated by J. B. Phillips. Copyright © 1972 by J. B. Phillips.

ISBN-13: 978-1-4335-0210-1
ISBN-10: 1-4335-0210-0
ePub ISBN: 978-1-4335-2201-7
PDF ISBN: 978-1-4335-0415-0
Mobipocket ISBN: 978-1-4335-0416-7

Library of Congress Cataloging-in-Publication Data

Packer, J. I. (James Innell)
   Affirming the Apostles' Creed / J. I. Packer.
      p.   cm.
   "This book was formerly part of Growing in Christ by J. I. Packer,
originally published under the title I want to be a Christian"—
T. p. verso.
   Includes bibliographical references.
   ISBN 978-1-4335-0210-1 (tpb)
   1. Apostles' Creed. I. Packer, J. I. (James Innell) Growing in
Christ. II. Title.
BT003.3.P33   2008
238'.11—dc22   2007045821

To

JIM, TOM,

AND ELISABETH

who by what they
are even more than
by what they say
share the strength they
have been given

Contents

The Apostles' Creed

I believe in God the Father almighty,
maker of heaven and earth;
and in Jesus Christ
his only Son our Lord,
who was conceived by the Holy Spirit,
born of the Virgin Mary,
suffered under Pontius Pilate,
was crucified, dead, and buried:
he descended into hell;
the third day he rose again from the dead;
he ascended into heaven,
and sitteth on the right hand of God the Father almighty;
from thence he shall come to judge the quick and the dead.
I believe in the Holy Spirit;
the holy catholic church;
the communion of saints;
the forgiveness of sins;
the resurrection of the body,
and the life everlasting.

If you are going to travel cross-country on foot, you need a map. Now there are different kinds of maps. One sort is the large-scale relief map, which marks all the paths, bogs, crags, and so on in detail. Since the walker needs the fullest information about his chosen route, he must have a map of that sort. But for choosing between the various ways he might go, he could well learn more, and more quickly, from a small-scale map that left out the detailed geography and just showed him the roads and trails leading most directly from one place to another. Well-prepared walkers have maps of both kinds.

If life is a journey, then the million-word-long Holy Bible is the large-scale map with everything in it, and the hundred-word Apostles' Creed (so called, not because apostles wrote it—despite later legend, they didn't—but because it teaches apostolic doctrine) is the simplified road map, ignoring much but enabling you to see at a glance the main points of Christian belief. *Creed* means "belief"; many Christians of former days used to call this Creed "the Belief," and in the second century, when it first appeared, almost as we have it now, it was called the Rule of Faith.

When folk inquire into Christianity, their advisers naturally want to get them studying the Bible and to lead them into personal trust in the living Christ as soon as they can, and rightly so. But as means to both ends, it helps to take them through the Creed, as both a preliminary orientation to the Bible and as a preliminary analysis of the convictions on which faith in Christ must rest.

Those convictions are Trinitarian. The Creed tells us of Father, Son, and Holy Spirit, so that having found out about them we might find them experientially. What do we learn from the Creed as we study it? The answer has been summarized beautifully as follows:

First, I learn to believe in God the Father, who hath made me, and all the world.

Secondly, in God the Son who hath redeemed me, and all mankind.

Thirdly, in God the Holy Ghost, who sanctifieth me, and all the elect people of God.[1]

When one has learned this much, one is not far from God's kingdom.

The purpose of knowledge is that we might apply it to life. This is nowhere truer than in Christianity, where true knowledge (knowledge of the true God) is precisely knowledge about God—applied. And knowledge about God, for application, is what is offered here, in the studies that follow.

NOTE

[1]The Prayer Book Catechism.

Weeklies for kids were well under way when I was young, and at age six or thereabouts I was devouring *Bubbles*. *Bubbles* brought me not only Dick the Boy Inventor, with his personal spaceship, and Val Fox and his Funny Pets, who every week helped Val detect crimes, but also puzzle drawings in which animals were hidden ("Can you find the elephant/lion/cat/cow in this picture?").

From the ridiculous, now, to the sublime: I want to press the question, can you find the gospel in the Apostles' Creed? And I want to display the Creed as, in effect, a power-point declaration of the basics of the Christian message—in other words, of the gospel itself.

Many today will react to that last sentence with skepticism. Why? Because of a habit that established itself in evangelistic circles in the twentieth century and became a mind-set among evangelicals generally. In the interests of memorable simplicity, evangelists, tract writers, youth workers, plus others boiled the gospel down to an ABC, commonly formulated as follows: (1) *a*ll have sinned and come short of the glory

of God, you included; (2) *b*elieve on the Lord Jesus Christ
and you will be saved; (3) *c*onfess Jesus Christ as the risen
Lord, and he will in due course welcome you into heaven. As
twentieth-century trains and cars came to be streamlined for
speed, so the gospel was streamlined for instant comprehension and response. The question being explored was: how
little do we need to tell people for them to become Christians?
Was this a good question to work with? In some circles,
maybe so, but in most, definitely not. Let me explain.

In North America, ever since the days of the Pilgrim
Fathers, a general idea of what constituted Christian belief
had been warp and woof in North American culture. Just as
sugar stirred into coffee is present in solution, so Christianity
was continuously present in solution in North American
culture right up to the twentieth century. Then, for a number
of reasons, Christianity and the Bible were eliminated from
public schools and universities, family prayer and Bible read-
ing at home closed down almost everywhere, a consciously
post-Christian and indeed anti-Christian outlook established
itself among thought leaders, and the gospel message had
to fight for entry into the minds of white people under fifty,
just as it had to do in the face of the paganism of the Roman
Empire in the apostolic and post-apostolic age. In such a
milieu, a truncated version of the gospel message, presenting
Christ the Redeemer apart from God the Creator, and remis-

sion of sins apart from personal regeneration, and individual salvation apart from life and worship in the church, and the hope of heaven apart from the pilgrim path of holiness—which is what in practice the ABC approach does—becomes a misrepresentation, one that sows the seed of many pastoral problems down the road. Against a background of general acquaintance with, and acceptance of, the Christian outlook, periodic highlighting of a few truths to galvanize response might not in itself be a bad idea; but when we reach the point where the Creed no longer looks or sounds to Christian people like a declaration of the gospel, there is need, I believe, for some whistle-blowing and reassessment of what goes on.

For in fact the Creed itself was born as an instrument of evangelism—first, as a summary syllabus for catechetical teaching of the faith to non-Jewish inquirers, and then as a declaration of personal faith for converts to use at the time of their baptism. Jewish converts in the days of the book of Acts, for whom the issue was simply acknowledging Jesus Christ as the long-awaited Messiah, were baptized in his name immediately on professing faith and brought straight into the fellowship of the church, but the initial discipling of pagan Gentiles required much more than that. So the catechumenate came into being. It seems that every congregation of any size in the second and third centuries had its ongoing instructional classes for teaching Christianity to those who wished to learn it. The course usually lasted three years and always climaxed with confession of faith and solemn baptism on Easter Eve, followed by first Eucharist on Easter Day. And the confession was made in the words of the Creed.

We should note as background that in the second century, when the Creed was crystallizing throughout the Christian world, the church was constantly harassed by sheep-stealing Gnostics. Their very name made an elitist boast; to catch the proud nuance of the Greek word *gnōstikoi*, you need to render it as "those in the know." And their Gnosticism was in fact an imaginative intellectualism that claimed to give the "real meaning" of each Christian doctrine, something that (so the Gnostics said) Christians regularly miss by reason of their mistaken idea that spirit and matter can interact to the point of uniting, and indeed have done so in the person of Jesus Christ.

The Gnostics posited two gods—a stupid and clumsy one who made all material things, including our bodies, and did not do it well and a wise and kindly one who is all spirit and is the source of our spirits currently inhabiting our bodies and who had taken steps to teach our spirits how finally to leave our bodies behind when we die and to make a beeline back to him and happiness. This is Christianity without Christ, a Hamlet-without-the-prince sort of thing. The Creed's sequence of topics, and some of its phrases, express not only apostolic teaching but also the explicit negation of Gnostic dualism at every point.

Look, now, at the doctrinal ground that the Creed, as syllabus, required catechumens to cover and, at introductory adult level, master.

(1) *The Trinity*. It is true that no explicit three-in-one formulations of the being of God are found in surviving Christian literature until the third and fourth centuries. But it is also true that the reality of the Father, the Son, and the Holy Spirit working together as a team for the full salvation of sinners pervades the entire New Testament. It is not too much to say that the gospel, which tells of the Son coming to earth, dying to redeem us, sending the Spirit to us, and finally coming in judgment, all at the Father's will, cannot be stated at all without speaking in an implicitly trinitarian way. "I believe in God the Father . . . and in Jesus Christ, his only Son, our Lord . . . and . . . in the Holy Ghost [Spirit]" gives the Creed a trinitarian shape for all its particular affirmations.

(2) *The creation*. The Creed starts with God as Maker of everything, including ourselves. "The Father Almighty" points to God's loving care for what he has made, and to his sovereign lordship over all of it. The Gnostics, who did not believe that the God who created is the God who redeems, are already being left behind.

(3) *The Incarnation*. The Son's course of stepping down,

or humiliation (virgin birth, crucifixion, death, and burial), followed by his step-by-step exaltation (resurrection, ascension, heavenly reign, future reign as royal judge), is spelled out in detail, for these facts are, after all, the heart of Christian faith. The virgin birth (which assumes the virginal conception, whereby the Son took flesh and became the God-man) is explicitly affirmed, and so is the reality of the Son's death. ("He descended into hell [Hades]," the place where all the departed go, is said to make the point that life left his body and he died as really, truly, and completely as you and I must expect in due course to do.) The reason for both these affirmations is not just their scripturalness and cruciality in the Christian story, but also the fact that the Gnostics made a point of denying them both.

The Gnostics negated the Incarnation as a monstrous mistake. They taught that a spirit, called the Christ, sent by the wise God to be our teacher, indwelt Jesus the man from his baptism to his final condemnation but then withdrew, leaving Jesus the man to suffer (or, as some said, to find a substitute for himself, so that he did not die). In any case, the Christ did not die, whatever may have happened to Jesus. Against this Christian teachers insisted from the start that a permanent union of divine and human took place in Mary's womb, that without diminishing his divinity the Son of God became man, died to rescue us from Satan, sin, and death, and now continues his incarnate life as the enthroned Lord of all and our eternal Savior-Judge.

(4) *The Holy Spirit.* The Pentecostal potentate, if we may reverently call him that, supernaturalizes believers' lives by both transforming their character into Christlikeness (so Paul and John show) and by shaping their circumstances, and their reactions to their circumstances, for kingdom advance (so Luke in Acts shows). Most of us need to catch up with what the catechumens would have been taught at this point.

(5) *The church.* Created and animated by the Holy Spirit, the church is the community of believers living through God and to God, the Father and the Son, in a sustained pattern of worship, work, and witness. (This is why the church is called "holy," which means set apart for God.) It is the world-wide people of God and body of Christ, in whose faith and fellowship social, racial, gender, age, educational, professional, and political distinctions cease to count; all are "one in Christ Jesus" (Galatians 3:28). (This is why the church is called "catholic," which means comprehensive, or inclusive, in both extent and quality.) Knowing and uniting with the Lord Jesus Christ according to the gospel is the dynamic basis of the church's inner unity and togetherness. So, no doubt, catechumens were taught, in the days when the Creed was first put together.

(6) *The forgiveness of sins.* In the Creed's order of instruc-

tion, this truth follows the account of the Holy Spirit, clearly because it is the Holy Spirit who makes us realize that sin, in its habits, acts, and guilt, is our problem and that until we get rid of its guilt we cannot have fellowship with God. Then the Spirit makes us realize that forgiveness, secured for us through Christ's atoning death, is God's free gift to us, which we receive through penitent faith (credence, consent, commitment) exercised toward Christ himself, the risen Lord. The gift is renewable; it is there to be received again and again, as often as we need it (which is, in fact, daily). And forgiveness of forsaken sins opens the door, every time, to new fellowship with our heavenly Father and with Jesus himself as our master and friend.

(7) *The Christian hope.* Gnostics anticipated disembodiment, but Christians look forward to being re-embodied, on the model of Jesus' resurrection, bodily ascension, and glorification. In the unending, unaging life with Jesus into which we shall enter, God's threefold purpose for bodies—namely, experience, enjoyment, and expression—will be fulfilled as never before.

Now I ask again: can you find the gospel in the Creed? And can you see that there is nothing in the Creed that is not part of the gospel, when fully stated? Today, on our own turf, we face pagan ignorance about God every bit as deep as that which the early church faced in the Roman Empire.

The ABC approach is thus not full enough; the whole story of the Father's Christ-exalting plan of redeeming love, from eternity to eternity, must be told, or the radical reorientation of life for which the gospel calls will not be understood, and the required total shift from man-centeredness to God-centeredness, and more specifically from self-centeredness to Christ-centeredness, will not take place. All that the Creed covers needs to be grasped and taught, as an integral part of the message of the saving love of God. To help in this is the purpose of the present book.

And without faith it is impossible to please him,
for whoever would draw near to God
must believe that he exists and that he rewards
those who seek him.

HEBREWS 11:6

I Believe in God

When people are asked what they believe in, they give not merely different answers, but different sorts of answers. Someone might say, "I believe in UFOs"—that means, "I think UFOs are real." "I believe in democracy"—that means, "I think democratic principles are just and beneficial." But what does it mean when Christian congregations stand and say, "I believe in God"? Far more than when the object of belief is UFOs or democracy.

I can believe in UFOs without ever looking for one and in democracy without ever voting. In cases like these, belief is a matter of the intellect only. But the Creed's opening words, "I believe in God," render a Greek phrase coined by the writers of the New Testament, meaning literally: "I *am believing into* God." That is to say, over and above believing certain truths *about* God, I am living in a relation of commitment *to* God in trust and union. When I say "I believe in God," I am professing my conviction that God has invited me to this commitment and declaring that I have accepted his invitation.

FAITH

The word *faith*, which is English for a Greek noun (*pistis*) formed from the verb in the phrase "believe into" (*pisteuo*), gets the idea of trustful commitment and reliance better than *belief* does. Whereas *belief* suggests bare opinion, *faith*, whether in a car, a patent medicine, a protégé, a doctor, a marriage partner, or what have you, is a matter of treating the person or thing as trustworthy and committing yourself accordingly. The same is true of faith in God, and in a more far-reaching way.

It is the offer and demand of the object that determines in each case what a faith-commitment involves. Thus, I show faith in my car by relying on it to get me places, and in my doctor by submitting to his treatment. And I show faith in God by bowing to his claim to rule and manage me; by receiving Jesus Christ, his Son, as my own Lord and Savior; and by relying on his promise to bless me here and hereafter. This is the meaning of response to the offer and demand of the God of the Creed.

*Christian faith only begins when we attend to
God's self-disclosure in Christ and in Scripture,
where we meet him as the Creator who
"commands all people everywhere to repent"
and to "believe in the name of his Son Jesus Christ."*

Sometimes faith is equated with that awareness of "one above" (or "beyond" or "at the heart of things") that from time to time, through the impact of nature, conscience, great art, being in love, or whatever, touches the hearts of the hardest-boiled. (Whether they take it seriously is another question, but it comes to all—God sees to that.) But Christian faith only begins when we attend to God's self-disclosure in Christ and in Scripture, where we meet him as the Creator who "commands all people everywhere to repent" and to "believe in the name of his Son Jesus Christ . . . as he has commanded us" (Acts 17:30; 1 John 3:23; cf. John 6:28ff.). Christian faith means hearing, noting, and doing what God says.

DOUBT

I write as if God's revelation in the Bible has self-evident truth and authority, and I think that in the last analysis it has; but I know, as you do, that uncriticized preconceptions and prejudices create problems for us all, and many have deep doubts and perplexities about elements of the biblical message. How do these doubts relate to faith?

Well, what is doubt? It is a state of divided mind— "double-mindedness" is James's concept (James 1:6–8)—and it is found both *within* faith and *without* it. In the former case, it is faith infected, sick, and out of sorts; in the latter, it belongs to a struggle either toward faith or away from a God felt to be invading and making claims one does not want to meet. In C. S. Lewis's spiritual autobiography *Surprised by Joy*, you can observe both these motivations successively.

In our doubts, we think we are honest, and certainly try to be; but perfect honesty is beyond us in this world, and an unacknowledged unwillingness to take God's word about things, whether from deference to supposed scholarship or fear of ridicule or of deep involvement or some other motive, often underlies a person's doubt about this or that item of faith. Repeatedly this becomes clear in retrospect, though we could not see it at the time.

How can one help doubters? First, by *explaining* the problem area (for doubts often arise from misunderstanding); second, by *exhibiting* the reasonableness of Christian belief at that point, and the grounds for embracing it (for Christian beliefs, though above reason, are not against it); third, by *exploring* what prompts the doubts (for doubts are never rationally compelling, and hesitations about Christianity usually have more to do with likes and dislikes, hurt feelings, and social, intellectual, and cultural snobbery than the doubters are aware).

PERSONAL

In worship, the Creed is said in unison, but the opening words are "I believe"—not "we": each worshiper speaks for himself. Thus he proclaims his philosophy of life and at the same time testifies to his happiness: he has come into the hands of the Christian God where he is glad to be, and when he says, "I believe," it is an act of praise and thanksgiving on his part. It is in truth a great thing to be able to say the Creed.

FURTHER BIBLE STUDY

Faith in action:

- Romans 4
- Hebrews 11
- Mark 5:25–34

QUESTIONS FOR THOUGHT AND DISCUSSION

- What is the essential meaning of *faith* (Greek *pistis*)?
- What is the importance of the word "I" in the Creed's opening phrase?
- What doubts about Christianity have you had to deal with in yourself and others?
- How can the approach outlined in this chapter help address doubts and questions we may have?

The LORD, the LORD, a God merciful and gracious, slow to anger, and abounding in steadfast love and faithfulness, keeping steadfast love for thousands, forgiving iniquity and transgression and sin.

EXODUS 34:6–7

CHAPTER 2

The God I Believe In

What should it mean when we stand in church and say, "I believe in God"? Are we at this point just allying ourselves with Jews, Moslems, Hindus, and others against atheism and declaring that there is some God as distinct from none? No; we are doing far more than this. We are professing faith in the God of the Creed itself, the Christian God, the God of the Bible—the Sovereign Creator whose "Christian name," as Karl Barth put it, is Father, Son, and Holy Spirit. If this is not the God in whom we believe, we have no business saying the Creed at all.

IDOLS

We must be clear here. Today's idea is that the great divide is between those who say "I believe in God" in some sense and those who cannot say it in any sense. Atheism is seen as an enemy, paganism is not, and it is assumed that the difference between one faith and another is quite secondary. But in the Bible the great divide is between those who believe in the Christian God and those who serve idols—"gods," that is, whose images, whether metal or mental, do not square with the self-disclosure of the Creator. One wishes that some who recite "I believe in God" in church each Sunday would see that what they actually mean is "I do *not* believe in God—not this God, anyhow!"

In the Bible the great divide is between those who believe in the Christian God and those who serve idols—"gods," that is, whose images, whether metal or mental, do not square with the self-disclosure of the Creator.

HIS NAME

The Bible tells us that God has revealed himself, establishing his identity, so to speak, by telling us his "name." This "name" appears in three connections.

First, God gave his "proper name," Jehovah (or Yahweh, as modern scholars prefer), to Moses at the burning bush (Exodus 3:13ff.; see also 6:3). The name means "I am who I am" or "I will be what I will be" (ESV, text and margin).

32

It declares God's almightiness: he cannot be hindered from being what he is and doing what he wills. Well did the AV translators render this name as "the LORD." The Creed echoes this emphasis when it speaks of God the Father *almighty*.

Second, God "proclaimed the name of the LORD" to Moses by delineating his moral character—"a God merciful and gracious, slow to anger, and abounding in steadfast love and faithfulness, keeping steadfast love for thousands, forgiving iniquity . . . but who will by no means clear the guilty" (Exodus 34:5–7). This "name"—you could call it a revealed description—discloses both God's *nature* and his *role*. It is a declaration whose echoes reverberate throughout the Bible (see Exodus 20:5ff.; Numbers 14:18; 2 Chronicles 30:9; Nehemiah 1:5; 9:17, 32; Psalm 86:5, 15; 103:8–18; 111:4–9; 112:4; 116:5; 145:8ff., 17, 20; Joel 2:13; Jonah 4:2; Romans 2:2–6), and all of God's acts that Scripture records confirm and illustrate its truth. It is noteworthy that when John focuses on the two sides of God's character by saying that he is both *light* and *love* (1 John 1:5; 4:8)— not love without righteousness and purity, nor rectitude without kindness and compassion, but holy love and loving holiness, and each quality to the highest degree—he offers each statement as summarizing what we learn from Jesus about God.

THREE IN ONE

Third, the Son of God told his disciples to baptize "in the name of the Father and of the Son and of the Holy Spirit" (Matthew 28:19). "Name," note, not "names": the three persons together constitute the one God. Here we face the most dizzying and unfathomable truth of all, the truth of the Trinity, to which the three paragraphs of the Creed (" the Father . . . his only Son . . . the Holy Spirit") also bear witness.

What should we make of this? In itself, the divine tri-unity is a mystery, a transcendent fact that passes our understanding. (The same is true of such realities as God's eternity, infinity, omniscience, and providential control of our free actions; indeed, all truths about God exceed our comprehension, more or less.) How the one eternal God is eternally both singular and plural, how Father, Son, and Spirit are personally distinct yet essentially one (so that tritheism, belief in three gods who are not one, and Unitarianism, belief in one God who is not three, are both wrong), is more than we can know, and any attempt to "explain" it—to dispel the mystery by reasoning, as distinct from confessing it from Scripture—is bound to falsify it. Here, as elsewhere, our God is too big for his creatures' little minds.

Yet the historical foundation-facts of Christian faith—a man who was God, praying to his Father and promising that he and his Father would send "another Helper" (John 14:16) to continue his divine ministry—and equally the universally experienced facts of Christian devotion—worshiping God the Father above you and knowing the fellowship of God the Son beside you, both through the prompting of God the Holy Spirit within you—point inescapably to God's essential three-in-oneness. So does the cooperative activity of the Three in saving us—the Father planning, the Son procuring, and the Spirit applying redemption. Many Scriptures witness to this: see, for instance, Romans 8:1–17; 2 Corinthians 13:14; Ephesians 1:3–14; 2 Thessalonians 2:13ff.; 1 Peter 1:2. When the gospel of Christ is analyzed, the truth of the Trinity proves to be its foundation and framework.

It was only through the work of grace, which centers on the Incarnation, that the one God was seen to be plural. No wonder, then, if those who do not believe in the work of grace doubt the truth of the Trinity too.

But this is the God of the Creed. Is this, now, the God whom we worship? Or have we too fallen victims to idolatry?

FURTHER BIBLE STUDY

God revealed:
• John 1:1–18

QUESTIONS FOR THOUGHT AND DISCUSSION

- What does it mean to say: "In the Bible the great divide is between those who believe in the Christian God and those who serve idols"? Do you agree or disagree? Why?
- What is the basic meaning of God's name Jehovah? What does it tell us about him?
- Why did Christ direct his disciples to baptize "in the name [singular] of the Father and of the Son and of the Holy Spirit"?

Have we not all one Father?
Has not one God created us?

MALACHI 2:10

CHAPTER 3

The Father Almighty

In any church where saying the Creed is part of the worship service it is likely that God's fatherhood will have been celebrated in song ("Glory be to the Father . . .") before the Creed is said, for it is a theme that with a sure instinct hymn-writers have always highlighted. But how should we understand it?

CREATION

Clearly, when the Creed speaks of "God the Father almighty, maker of heaven and earth," it has in immediate view the fact that we and all things besides depend on God as Creator for our existence, every moment. Now to call creatorship fatherhood is not unscriptural: it echoes both the Old Testament—Malachi 2:10, "Have we not all one Father? Has not one God created us?"—and the New Testament—Acts 17:28, where

Paul preaching at Athens quotes with approval a Greek poet's statement: "we are indeed his offspring." Nonetheless, both these quotations come from passages threatening divine judgment, and Paul's evangelistic sermon at Athens makes it very clear that though the offspring relationship implies an obligation to seek, worship, and obey God and makes one answerable to him at the end of the day, it does not imply his favor and acceptance where repentance for past sins and faith in Christ are lacking (see the whole speech, verses 22–31).

Some who stress the universal fatherhood of God treat it as implying that all men are and always will be in a state of salvation, but that is not the biblical view. Paul speaks of persons to whom "the word of the cross is folly" as "perishing" (1 Corinthians 1:18) and warns the "impenitent" that "you are storing up wrath for yourself on the day of wrath" (Romans 2:5), however much they are God's offspring.

FATHER AND SON

In fact, when the New Testament speaks of God's fatherhood it is not with reference to creation, but in two further connections. The first is *the inner life of the Godhead*. Within the eternal Trinity is a family relation of Father and Son. On earth, the Son called the One whom he served "my Father" and prayed to him as Abba—the Aramaic equivalent of a respectful Dad.

What this relationship meant Jesus himself declared. On the one hand, the Son loves the Father (John 14:31) and always does what pleases the Father (8:29). He takes no initiatives, depending instead every moment on the Father for a lead (5:19ff., 30), but he is tenacity itself in cleaving to the Father's known will. "My Father . . . not as I will, but as you will . . . your will be done" (Matthew 26:39, 42). "Shall I not drink the cup that the Father has given me?" (John 18:11).

God's loving fatherhood of his eternal Son is both the archetype of his gracious relationship with his own redeemed people and the model from which derives the parenthood that God has created in human families.

On the other hand, the Father loves the Son (John 3:35; 5:20) and makes him great by giving him glory and great things to do (5:20–30; 10:17ff.; 17:23–26). Giving life and executing judgment are twin tasks that have been wholly committed to him, "that all may honor the Son" (5:23).

God's loving fatherhood of his eternal Son is both the archetype of his gracious relationship with his own redeemed people and the model from which derives the parenthood that God has created in human families. Paul spoke of "the God and Father of our Lord Jesus Christ" as "the Father, from whom every family in heaven and on earth is named" (Ephesians 1:3; 3:14ff.). Human families, by their very constitution, reflect the Father-Son relationship in heaven, and parent-child relationships should express a love that corresponds to the mutual love of Father and Son in the Godhead.

ADOPTION

The second connection in which the New Testament speaks of God as Father has to do with *the believing sinner's adoption* into the life of God's family. This is a supernatural gift of grace, linked with justification and new birth, given freely by God and received humbly by faith in Jesus Christ as Savior and Lord. "To all who did receive him [Jesus], who believed in his name, he gave power to become children of God, who were born . . . of God" (John 1:12ff.). The message Jesus sent to his disciples on rising from the dead was: "I am ascending to my Father and your Father, to my God and your God" (John 20:17). As disciples, they belonged to the family; indeed, in that very sentence Jesus called them "my brothers." All whom he has saved are his brothers.

When the Christian says the first clause of the Creed, he will put all this together and confess his Creator as both the Father of his Savior and his own Father through Christ—a

Father who now loves him no less than he loves his only begotten Son. That is a marvelous confession to be able to make.

ALMIGHTY

And God the Father is "almighty"—which means that he can and will do all that he intends. What does he intend for his sons? Answer: that they should share all that their elder Brother enjoys now. Believers are "heirs of God and fellow heirs with Christ, provided we suffer with him in order that we may also be glorified with him" (Romans 8:17). Suffer we shall, but we shall not miss the glory: the Father almighty will see to that. Praise his name.

FURTHER BIBLE STUDY

On our adoption in Christ:

- Ephesians 1:3–14
- Galatians 4:1–7

QUESTIONS FOR THOUGHT AND DISCUSSION

- What does the statement "we are indeed his offspring" say about God's fatherhood? What does it leave out?
- How is God's fatherhood seen within the Trinity?
- Why can Jesus call Christians his "brothers"?

Whatever the Lord pleases,
he does, in heaven and on earth,
in the seas and all deeps.

PSALM 135:6

CHAPTER 4

Almighty

The Creed declares faith in "God the Father *almighty*." Does the adjective matter? Yes, a great deal. It points to the basic Bible fact that God is the Lord, the King, the omnipotent one who reigns over his world. Note the ecstatic joy with which God's sovereign rule is proclaimed and praised in (for instance) Psalms 93, 96, 97, 99:1–5, and 103. Men treat God's sovereignty as a theme for controversy, but in Scripture it is matter for worship.

We need to realize that you cannot rightly understand God's ways at any point until you see them in the light of his sovereignty. That, no doubt, is why the Creed takes the first opportunity of announcing it. But though the believing heart warms to it, it is not an easy truth for our minds to grasp, and a number of questions arise.

WHAT GOD CANNOT DO

First, does omnipotence mean that God can do literally anything? No, that is not the meaning. There are many things God cannot do. He cannot do what is self-contradictory or nonsensical, like squaring the circle. Nor (and this is vital) can he act out of character. God has a perfect moral character, and it is not in him to deny it. He cannot be capricious, unloving, random, unjust, or inconsistent. Just as he cannot pardon sin without atonement, because that would not be right, so he cannot fail to be "faithful and just" in forgiving sins that are confessed in faith and in keeping all the other promises he has made, for failure here would not be right either. Moral instability, vacillation, and unreliability are marks of weakness, not of strength: but God's omnipotence is supreme strength, making it impossible that he should lapse into imperfections of this sort.

The positive way to say this is that though there are things that a holy, rational God is incapable of intending, all that he intends to do he actually does. "Whatever the Lord pleases, he does" (Psalm 135:6). As, when he planned to make the world, "he spoke, and it came to be" (Psalm 33:9; see Genesis 1), so it is with each other thing that he wills. With men, "there's many a slip 'twixt cup and lip," but not with him.

HUMAN FREE WILL

Second, is not God's power to fulfill his purposes limited by the free will of man? No. Man's power of spontaneous and responsible choice is a created thing, an aspect of the mystery of created human nature, and God's power to fulfill his purposes is not limited by anything that he has made. Just as he works out his will through the functioning of the physical order, so he works out his will through the functioning of our psychological makeup. In no case is the integrity of the created thing affected, and it is always possible (apart from some miracles) to "explain" what has happened without reference to the rule of God. But in every case God orders the things that come to pass.

So, therefore, without violating the nature of created realities, or reducing man's activity to robot level, God still "works all things according to the counsel of his will" (Ephesians 1:11).

But surely in that case what we think of as our free will is illusory and unreal? That depends on what you mean. It is certainly illusory to think that our wills are only free if they operate apart from God. But free will in the sense of "free agency," as theologians have defined it—that is, the power of spontaneous, self-determining choice referred to above— is real. As a fact of creation, an aspect of our humanness, it exists, as all created things do, in God. How God sustains it and overrules it without overriding it is his secret; but that he does so is certain, both from our conscious experience of making decisions and acting "of our own free will," and also from Scripture's sobering insistence that we are answerable to God for our actions, just because in the moral sense they really are ours.

EVIL IS MASTERED

Third, does not the existence of evil—moral badness, useless pain, and waste of good—suggest that God the Father is not almighty after all, for surely he would remove these things if he could? Yes, he would, and he is doing so! Through Christ, bad folk like you and me are already being made good; new pain- and disease-free bodies are on the way, and a reconstructed cosmos with them; and Paul assures us that "the sufferings of this present time are not worth comparing with the glory that is to be revealed to us" (Romans 8:18; cf. verses 19–23). If God moves more slowly than we wish in clearing evil out of his world and introducing the new order, that, we may be sure, is in order to widen his gracious purpose and include in it more victims of the world's evil than otherwise he could have done. (Study 2 Peter 3:3–10, especially verse 8ff.)

The truth of God's almightiness in creation, providence,
and grace is the basis of all our trust, peace, and
joy in God, and the safeguard of all our hopes
of answered prayer, present protection,
and final salvation.

GOOD NEWS

The truth of God's almightiness in creation, providence, and grace is the basis of all our trust, peace, and joy in God, and the safeguard of all our hopes of answered prayer, present protection, and final salvation. It means that neither fate, nor the stars, nor blind chance, nor man's folly, nor Satan's malice controls this world; instead, a morally perfect God runs it, and none can dethrone him or thwart his purposes of love. And if I am Christ's, then—

A sovereign protector I have,
Unseen, yet forever at hand,
Unchangeably faithful to save,
Almighty to rule and command. . . .

If thou art my Shield and my Sun
The night is no darkness to me,
And, fast as my moments roll on,
They bring me but nearer to thee.

Good news? Yes, the best ever.

FURTHER BIBLE STUDY

God the overruler:
- Genesis 50:15–26
- Psalm 93
- Acts 4:23–31

QUESTIONS FOR THOUGHT AND DISCUSSION

- What does "almighty" mean? Why is it important to believe that God is almighty?
- In what sense, if any, is it true to say there are some things that even omnipotence cannot do?
- Is God's power limited by man's free will? Why or why not?

For everything created by God is good,
and nothing is to be rejected if it is received
with thanksgiving.

1 TIMOTHY 4:4

CHAPTER 5

Maker of Heaven and Earth

In the beginning, God created the heavens and the earth"; so begins the Bible. ("The heavens and the earth" is Bible language for "everything that is.")

It is arguable how much (or how little) Genesis 1 and 2 tell us about the *method* of creation—whether, for instance, they do or do not rule out the idea of physical organisms evolving through epochs of thousands of years. What is clear, however, is that their main aim is to tell us not how the world was made but who made it.

INTRODUCING THE ARTIST

The solution-chapter in one of Dorothy Sayers's detective stories is called "When You Know How You Know Who."

Genesis 1 and 2, however, tell us *who* without giving many answers about *how*. Some today may think this a defect; but in the long perspective of history our present-day "scientific" preoccupation with *how* rather than *who* looks very odd in itself. Rather than criticize these chapters for not feeding our secular interest, we should take from them needed rebuke of our perverse passion for knowing Nature without regard for what matters most—namely, knowing Nature's Creator.

The message of these two chapters is this: "You have seen the sea? The sky? The sun, moon, and stars? You have watched the birds and the fish? You have observed the landscape, the vegetation, the animals, the insects, all the big things and little things together? You have marveled at the wonderful complexity of human beings, with all their powers and skills, and the deep feelings of fascination, attraction, and affection that men and women arouse in each other? Fantastic, isn't it? Well now, meet the one who is behind it all!" As if to say: now that you have enjoyed these works of art, you must shake hands with the artist; since you were thrilled by the music, we will introduce you to the composer. It was to show us the Creator rather than the creation, and to teach us knowledge of God rather than physical science, that Genesis 1 and 2, along with such celebrations of creation as Psalm 104 and Job 38–41, were written.

In creating, God was craftsman and more. Craftsmen

shape existing material and are limited by it, but no material existed at all until God said, "Let there be . . ." To make this point theologians speak of creation "out of nothing," meaning not that nothing was a sort of a something(!) but that God in creating was absolutely free and unrestricted, and that nothing determined or shaped what he brought into being save his own idea of what it would be like.

CREATOR AND CREATURE

The Creator-creature distinction is basic to the Bible's view of God's lordship in providence and grace, and indeed to all true thought about God and man. That is why it is in the Creed. Its importance is at least threefold.

First, *it stops misunderstanding of God*. God made us in his image, but we tend to think of him in ours! ("Man made God in his own image" was a crack by Voltaire, rather too true to be good.) But the Creator-creature distinction reminds us that God does not depend on us as we depend on him, nor does he exist by our will and for our pleasure, nor may we think of his personal life as being just like ours. As creatures we are limited; we cannot know everything at once, nor be present everywhere, nor do all we would like to do, nor continue unchanged through the years. But the Creator is not limited in these ways. Therefore we find him *incomprehensible*—by which I mean, not *making no sense*, but *exceeding our grasp*. We can no more take his measure than our dogs and cats can take our measure. When Luther told Erasmus that his thoughts of God were *too human*, he was uprooting in principle all the rationalistic religion that has ever infected the church—and rightly too! We must learn to be self-critical in our thinking about God.

 The world exists in its present stable state by the will and power of its Maker. Since it is his world, we are not its owners, free to do as we like with it, but its stewards, answerable to him for the way we handle its resources.

Second, *this distinction stops misunderstanding of the world.* The world exists in its present stable state by the will and power of its Maker. Since it is his world, we are not its owners, free to do as we like with it, but its stewards, answerable to him for the way we handle its resources. And since it is his world, we must not depreciate it. Much religion has built on the idea that the material order—reality as experienced through the body, along with the body that experiences it—is evil and therefore to be refused and ignored as far as possible. This view, which dehumanizes its devotees, has sometimes called itself Christian, but it is really as un-Christian as can be. For matter, being made by God, was and is *good* in his eyes

(Genesis 1:31) and so should be so in ours (1 Timothy 4:4). We serve God by using and enjoying temporal things gratefully, with a sense of their value to him, their Maker, and of his generosity in giving them to us. It is an ungodly and, indeed, inhuman super-spirituality that seeks to serve the Creator by depreciating any part of his creation.

Third, *this distinction stops misunderstanding of ourselves.* As man is not his own maker, so he may not think of himself as his own master. "God made me for himself, to serve him here." God's claim upon us is the first fact of life that we must face, and we need a healthy sense of our creaturehood to keep us facing it.

FURTHER BIBLE STUDY

God the Creator:
- Genesis 1–2
- Isaiah 45:9–25

QUESTIONS FOR THOUGHT AND DISCUSSION

- What is the significance of God's words "Let there be . . ."?
- What does the Creator-creature distinction have to do with God making man in his own image?
- Why can we say with confidence that the material order is not evil?

And the Word became flesh and dwelt among us,
and we have seen his glory, glory as of the
only Son from the Father, full of grace
and truth.

JOHN 1:14

CHAPTER 6

And in Jesus Christ

I believe in God the Father . . . and in Jesus Christ his only Son our Lord." So the Creed declares. When it called God "maker of heaven and earth," it parted company with Hinduism and Eastern faiths generally; now, by calling Jesus Christ God's only Son, it parts company with Judaism and Islam and stands quite alone. This claim for Jesus is both the touchstone of Christianity and the ingredient that makes it unique. As the whole New Testament was written to make and justify the claim, we should not be surprised when we find the Creed stating it with fuller detail than it states anything else.

CHRIST AND THE CENTER

This claim is central to the layout of the Creed, for the long section on Jesus Christ stands between the two shorter sections on the Father and the Spirit. And it is central to the faith of the Creed, for we could not know about the Trinity or salvation or resurrection and life everlasting apart from Jesus Christ. It was Jesus Christ, in his redemption of all God's people, who was the revealer of all these truths.

See how the Creed presents him.

Jesus (Greek for Joshua, meaning "God is Savior") is his proper name. It identifies him as a historical person, Mary's son from Nazareth in Galilee, a Jewish ex-carpenter who worked for three years as a rural rabbi and was put to death by the Roman authorities about A.D. 30. The four Gospels describe his ministry in some detail.

Christ (literally, "the anointed one") is not a surname, except in the old sense in which surnames like Smith, Taylor, Packer, or Clark declared a man's trade or profession. "Christ" is what Presbyterians would call an "office-title," identifying Jesus as God's appointed savior-king for whom the Jews had long been waiting. Since the Christ was expected to set up God's reign and to be hailed as overlord throughout the world, to call Jesus *Christ* was to claim for him a decisive place in history and a universal dominion that all men everywhere must acknowledge. The first Christians did this quite self-consciously; one sees them doing it in the speeches recorded in Acts (see 2:22–36; 3:12–26; 5:29–32; 10:34–43; 13:26–41; etc.). "To this end Christ died and lived again, that he might be Lord both of the dead and of the living" (Romans 14:9). ". . . so that at the name of Jesus every knee should bow" (Philippians 2:10).

Also, the title *Christ* expresses the claim that Jesus fulfilled all three ministries for which men were anointed in Old Testament times, being *prophet* (a messenger from God) and *priest* (one who mediates with God for us by sacrifice) as well as being *king*.

The glory of this conjunction of roles is only seen when we relate it to our actual needs. What do we sinners need for a right and good relationship with God? First, we are ignorant of him and need instruction, for no satisfying relationship is possible with a person about whom you know little or nothing. Second, we are estranged from him and need reconciliation—otherwise we shall end up unaccepted, unforgiven, and unblessed, strangers to his fatherly love and exiles from the inheritance that is in store for those who are his children. Third, we are weak, blind, and foolish when it comes to the business of living for God, and we need someone to guide, protect, and strengthen us, which is how the regal role was understood in Old Testament Israel. Now in the person and ministry of the one man, Jesus Christ, this threefold need is completely and perfectly met! Hallelujah!

Great Prophet of my God!
My tongue would bless thy name;
By thee the joyful news
Of our salvation came;
The joyful news of sins forgiven,
Of hell subdued, and peace with heaven.

Jesus, my great High Priest,
Offered his blood and died;
My guilty conscience seeks
No sacrifice beside;
His powerful blood did once atone,
And now it pleads before the throne.

My dear Almighty Lord,
My conqueror and my King,
Thy sceptre, and thy sword,
Thy reigning grace I sing.
Thine is the power; behold, I sit
In willing bonds before thy feet.

THE DIVINE LORD

Jesus, who is the Christ (says the Creed), is God's *only Son*. This identifies Mary's boy as the second person of the eternal Trinity, the Word who was the Father's agent in making the world and sustaining it right up to the present (John 1:1–4; Colossians 1:13–20; Hebrews 1:1–3). Staggering? Yes, certainly, but this identification is the heart of Christianity. "The word of God became a human being and lived among us" (John 1:14, *Phillips*).

If Jesus is God the Son, our co-creator, and is also Christ, the anointed savior-king, now risen from death and reigning in the place of authority and power, then he has a right to rule us, and we have no right to resist his claim.

"Our Lord" follows straight from this. If Jesus is God the Son, our co-creator, and is also Christ, the anointed savior-king, now risen from death and reigning (sitting, as the Creed puts it, "on the right hand of God the Father almighty," in the place of authority and power), then he has a right to rule us, and we have no right to resist his claim. As he invaded space and time in Palestine nearly two thousand years ago, so he invades our personal space and time today, with the same purpose of love that first brought him to earth. "Come, follow me" was his word then, and it is so still.

Is he, then, your Lord? For all who say the Creed, this question is inescapable; for how can you say "our Lord" in church until you have first said "my Lord" in your heart?

FURTHER BIBLE STUDY

Jesus—God and man:

• Hebrews 1:1—3:6

QUESTIONS FOR THOUGHT AND DISCUSSION

- What is the significance, historically and for us today, of the name *Jesus*?
- What should the title *Christ* have meant to a waiting Jewish nation? What should it mean to us?
- Why can Christ rightfully claim authority to rule your life?

A voice from the cloud said,
"This is my beloved Son, with whom
I am well pleased; listen to him."

MATTHEW 17:5

CHAPTER 7

His Only Son

When you hear a young man introduced as "my only son," you know he is the apple of his father's eye. The words reveal affection. When the Creed calls Jesus God's "only Son" (echoing "only begotten" in John 1:18; 3:16, 18, KJV), the implication is the same. Jesus, as God's only Son, enjoys his Father's dearest love. God said so himself when speaking from heaven to identify Jesus at his baptism and transfiguration: "This is my beloved Son . . ." (Matthew 3:17; 17:5).

FULLY GOD

Moreover, this phrase of the Creed is a bulwark against such lowering and denial of Jesus' deity as one finds in Unitarianism and the cults. Jesus was not just a God-inspired good man. Nor was he a super-angel, first and finest of all creatures, called "god" by courtesy because he is far above men (which is what

Arians said in the fourth century and Jehovah's Witnesses say today). Jesus was, and remains, God's only Son, as truly and fully God as his Father is. God's will, said Jesus, is "that all may honor the Son, just as they honor the Father" (John 5:23), a statement that knocks Unitarianism flat.

Jesus was not just a God-inspired good man.
Nor was he a super-angel, first and finest of all
creatures, called "god" by courtesy because he is
far above men. Jesus was, and remains, God's only
Son, as truly and fully God as his Father is.

But is it not mere mythology to talk of a Father-Son relationship within the Godhead? No, for Jesus himself talked this way. He called God "my Father" and himself not "*a*" but "*the* Son." He spoke of a unique and eternal Father-Son relation, into which he had come to bring others. "No one knows the Father except the Son and anyone to whom the Son chooses to reveal him" (Matthew 11:27).

BEGOTTEN

"Begotten of his Father before all worlds . . . begotten, not made," says the Nicene Creed. This is the language of fourth-century debate. The point of it is that though the Son lives his life in dependence on the Father, because that is his nature

("I live because of the Father," John 6:57), he is in himself divine and eternal and is not a created being. The phrase is not suggesting that the Son originated after the Father or is in himself less than the Father.

"Begotten" in John's phrase "only begotten" cannot signify an event in God's past that is not also part of his present, since it is only for us creatures who live in time that momentary events exist. Time as we know it is part of creation, and its Maker is not subject to its limitations, any more than he is subject to the limitations of created space. For us, life is a sequence of moments, and future and past events (begettings or any other) are both out of reach; but to God (so we must suppose, though we cannot imagine it) all events are constantly present in an eternal Now.

So the pre-mundane "begetting" of the Son (as distinct from the temporal and metaphorical "begetting" of the king in Psalm 2:7, which is applied to Christ in Acts 13:33 and Hebrews 1:5; 5:5, and which means simply bringing him to the throne) must be thought of not as a momentary event whereby God, after being singular, became plural, but as an eternal relationship whereby the first person is always Father to the Son and the second is always Son to the Father. In the third century Origen happily expressed this thought by speaking of the "eternal generation" of the Son. This is part of the unique glory of the triune God.

MYSTERY

Formulae for the Incarnation—the Council of Chalcedon's "one person in two natures, fully God and fully man" or Karl Barth's "God for man, and man for God"—sound simple, but the thing itself is unfathomable. It is easy to shoot down the ancient heresies that the Son took a human body without a human soul or that he was always two persons under one skin, and with them the modern heresy that the "enfleshing" of the Son was merely a special case of the indwelling of the Spirit, so that Jesus was not God but merely a God-filled man. But to grasp what the Incarnation was in positive terms is beyond us. Don't worry, though; you do not need to know how God became man in order to know Christ! Understand it or not, the fact remains that "the Word became flesh" (John 1:14); that was the supreme, mind-blowing miracle. Love prompted it; and our part is not to speculate about it and scale it down but to wonder and adore and love and exalt "Jesus Christ . . . the same yesterday and today and forever" (Hebrews 13:8).

Answer thy mercy's whole design,
My God incarnated for me;
My spirit make thy radiant shrine,
My light and full salvation be;
And through the shades of death unknown
Conduct me to thy dazzling throne.

FURTHER BIBLE STUDY

God's incarnate Son:

• Colossians 1:13–23

QUESTIONS FOR THOUGHT AND DISCUSSION

• Why is it not enough to call Jesus God-inspired, a superior angel, or even a god?

• What is the significance of the fact that the Son is not a created being?

• Why does facing Christianity mean facing up to Jesus Christ?

Behold, the virgin shall conceive
and bear a son, and shall call his name
Immanuel.

ISAIAH 7:14

CHAPTER 8

Born of the Virgin Mary

The Bible says that the Son of God entered and left this world by acts of supernatural power. His exit was by resurrection-plus-ascension, and his entry by virgin birth, both fulfilling Old Testament anticipations (see Isaiah 7:14 for the virgin birth and 53:10–12 for resurrection-ascension).

The entry and exit miracles carry the same message. First, they confirm that Jesus, though not less than man, was more than man. His earthly life, though fully human, was also divine. He, the co-creator, was in this world—his own world—as a visitor; he came from God and went to God.

The Fathers appealed to the virgin birth as proof not that Jesus was truly divine as distinct from being merely human, but that he was truly human as distinct from merely looking human as ghosts and angels might do, and it was probably as a witness against *docetism* (as this view was called) that the virgin birth was included in the Creed. But it witnesses against *humanitarianism* (the view that Jesus was just a fine man) with equal force.

Second, these two miracles indicate Jesus' freedom from sin. Virgin-born, he did not inherit the guilty twist called original sin: his manhood was untainted, and his acts, attitudes, motives, and desires were consequently faultless. The New Testament emphasizes his sinlessness (see John 8:29, 46; Romans 5:18ff.; 2 Corinthians 5:21; Hebrews 4:15; 7:26; 1 Peter 2:22–24; etc.). Being sinless, he could not be held by death once his sacrifice was done.

Two Stories

The New Testament gives two complementary accounts of the virgin birth, evidently independent yet strikingly harmonious—Joseph's story in Matthew 1 and Mary's in Luke 1–2. Both show every sign of being sober history. Ancient historians, seeing themselves as artists and moralists, usually omitted reference to sources, but Luke drops a broad hint that he had received Mary's narrative firsthand (cf. 2:51 with 1:1–3).

Matthew and Luke give two genealogies of Jesus (Matthew

1:2–17; Luke 3:23–38), which has puzzled some, but there are at least two straightforward ways of harmonizing them. Either Luke's genealogy gives Mary's line but starts with Joseph as Jesus' putative father (verse 23) because it was standard practice to declare descent through males, or else Luke traces Joseph's biological descent as distinct from the royal line of succession that Matthew appears to follow throughout. (See Professor F. F. Bruce, "Genealogy of Jesus Christ," in *The New Bible Dictionary* for the details.)

SKEPTICISM

For the past century and a half skepticism about both Jesus' virgin birth and his physical resurrection has been quite unreasonably strong. It began as part of a rationalistic quest for a non-miraculous Christianity, and though that quest is now out of fashion (and a good thing too) the skepticism lingers on, clinging to the minds of Christian people as the smell of cigarettes clings to the room after the ashtrays have been cleared. It is no doubt possible (though it is neither easy nor natural) to believe in the incarnation of the eternal, preexisting Son while disbelieving the entry and exit miracles; greater inconsistencies have been known. But it is much more logical, indeed the only reasonable course, to hold that since on other grounds we acknowledge Jesus and the Word made flesh, these two miracles, as elements in the larger miracle of the Son's incarnate life, raise no special difficulty.

Certainly, if we deny the virgin birth because it was a miracle, we should in logic deny Jesus' bodily resurrection too. These miracles are on a par, and it is unreasonable to accept either while rejecting the other.

Mary was a virgin until after Jesus' birth, but later ideas of her perpetual virginity are merely fanciful. The Gospels show that Jesus had brothers and sisters (Mark 3:31; 6:3).

If we deny the virgin birth because it was a miracle, we should in logic deny Jesus' bodily resurrection too. These miracles are on a par, and it is unreasonable to accept either while rejecting the other.

"Conceived by the Holy Spirit, born of the Virgin Mary" in the Creed witnesses to the reality of the Incarnation, not the glory of Jesus' mother. The Roman Catholic Church, however, has sponsored the unhappy development of Mariology (Mary-doctrine) among theologians and Mariolatry (Mary-worship) among the faithful. Mariology, which sees Mary as co-redeemer, rests on the non-biblical teaching that Mary, like Jesus, was born without sin (the immaculate conception) and entered resurrection glory straight after death (the assumption).

But the real Mary, the Mary of Scripture, saw herself simply as a saved sinner. "My spirit hath rejoiced in God my Saviour" (Luke 1:47, KJV). She sets us a marvelous example, not just of the privilege (and the price!) of cooperating in God's plan to bless the world (see Luke 1:38; 2:34–35), but also of humble response to God's grace. Parents are slow to take things from their children, and Jesus himself commented sadly at one stage that "a prophet is not without honor except . . . in his own household" (Matthew 13:57); but Mary and her family, after initial disbelief (cf. Matthew 13:57; Mark 3:20ff., 31–35; John 7:3–5), came to living faith in her son (Acts 1:14). Have we learned from their example?

FURTHER BIBLE STUDY

The virgin birth:
- Matthew 1:1–25   • Luke 1:26–56

QUESTIONS FOR THOUGHT AND DISCUSSION

- What do the miracles associated with Christ's earthly entry and exit show us about him?
- Do you agree that one's attitude toward the virgin birth and the resurrection of Jesus should be the same?
- How does the biblical picture of Mary compare with that traditionally given by the Roman Catholic Church?

All we like sheep have gone astray;
we have turned—every one—to his own way;
and the Lord has laid on him the
iniquity of us all.

ISAIAH 53:6

CHAPTER 9

Suffered under Pontius Pilate

Fancy a school of scientists or philosophers, or the members of a political party, constantly repeating that their founder was put to death by the government as a threat to law and order! Yet this is what Christians do, and the cross of Jesus is the centerpiece of the Creed. "Suffered under Pontius Pilate, was crucified." Look at these words in reverse order.

"Was crucified." This was the standard Roman way of executing criminals. To say "Jesus was crucified" is like saying he was hanged or went to the electric chair.

PILATE

"Under Pontius Pilate." Hitler will be remembered as the man who gassed the Jews, and Pilate, a nonentity otherwise, goes down in history as the man who killed Jesus. Under the Roman occupation, the Jewish authorities could not execute anyone; so when they had passed sentence on Jesus for confessing his true identity as God's Savior-King, the Christ (they thought the confession blasphemous), they passed him on to the governor for action.

Pilate, having symbolically washed his hands of the matter—the goofiest gesture, perhaps, of all time—gave the green light for judicial murder, directing that Jesus, though guiltless, should die all the same to keep people happy. Pilate saw this as shrewd government; how cynical can you get?

PASSION

"Suffered." This word carries not only the everyday meaning of bearing pain, but also the older and wider sense of being the object affected by someone else's action. The Latin is *passus*, whence the noun *passion*. Both God and men were agents of Jesus' passion: "this Jesus, delivered up according to the definite plan and foreknowledge of God, you crucified and killed by the hands of lawless men" (Acts 2:23, from Peter's first sermon). God's purpose at the cross was as real as was the guilt of the crucifiers.

*Jesus knew on the cross all the pain, physical and
mental, that man could inflict and also the divine
wrath and rejection that my sins deserve; for he was
there in my place, making atonement for me.*

What was God's purpose? Judgment on sin, for the sake
of mercy to sinners. The miscarrying of human justice was
the doing of divine justice. Jesus knew on the cross all the
pain, physical and mental, that man could inflict and also the
divine wrath and rejection that my sins deserve; for he was
there in my place, making atonement for me. "All we like
sheep have gone astray . . . and the LORD has laid on him the
iniquity of us all" (Isaiah 53:6).

> *Because the sinless Saviour died*
> *My sinful soul is counted free;*
> *For God, the Just, is satisfied*
> *To look on him—and pardon me.*

PROPITIATION

Here we reach the real heart—the heart of the heart, we may
say—of Christianity; for if the Incarnation is its shrine, the
Atonement is certainly its holy of holies. If the Incarnation
was the supreme miracle, it was yet only the first of a series of
steps down from the joy and bliss of heaven to the pain and
shame of Calvary (Philippians 2:5–8). The reason why the Son

of God became man was to shed his blood as (in the Prayer Book's words) "a full, perfect, and sufficient sacrifice, oblation, and satisfaction, for the sins of the whole world." God "did not spare his own Son but gave him up for us all" (Romans 8:32): that was the measure of his love (cf. Romans 5:5–8).

It is in the same terms—terms, that is, not of tolerant avuncular benevolence but of this particular precious gift— that John explains what he means by his great and glorious, but much-misunderstood, declaration, "*God is love.*" "In this is love," he explains, "not that we loved God but that [when we didn't] he loved us and sent his Son to be the expiation [better, propitiation] for our sins" (1 John 4:8–10).

The cross of Christ has many facets of meaning. As our sacrifice for sins, it was *propitiation* (Romans 3:25; 1 John 2:2; 4:10; cf. Hebrews 2:17)—that is, a means of quenching God's personal penal wrath against us by blotting out our sins from his sight. ("Expiation" in the RSV rendering of these texts signifies only "a means of blotting out sins," which is an inadequate translation.) As our propitiation, it was *reconciliation*, the making of peace for us with our offended, estranged, angry Creator (Romans 5:9–11). We are not wise to play down God's hostility against us sinners; what we should do is magnify our Savior's achievement for us in displacing wrath by peace.

Again, as our reconciliation, the cross was *redemption*,

rescue from bondage and misery by the payment of a price (see Ephesians 1:7; Romans 3:24; Revelation 5:9; Mark 10:45); and as redemption, it was *victory* over all hostile powers that had kept us, and wanted still to keep us, in sin and out of God's favor (Colossians 2:13–15). All these angles must be explored if we are to grasp the whole truth.

"The Son of God . . . loved me and gave himself for me"; so "God forbid that I should glory, save in the cross of our Lord Jesus Christ" (Galatians 2:20; 6:14, KJV). So said Paul. Thank God, I can identify. Can you?

FURTHER BIBLE STUDY

The meaning of the cross:
- Isaiah 53   • Romans 3:19–26   • Hebrews 10:1–25

QUESTIONS FOR THOUGHT AND DISCUSSION

- What is the full meaning that Christians find in the word "suffered" (Latin *passus*)?
- "Both God and men were agents of Jesus' passion." Explain.
- What does Christ's death have to do with your sins?

For Christ also suffered once for sins,

the righteous for the unrighteous,

that he might bring us to God,

being put to death in the flesh

but made alive in the spirit.

1 PETER 3:18

CHAPTER 10

He Descended into Hell

D eath has been called "the new obscenity," the nasty thing that no polite person nowadays will talk about in public. But death, even when unmentionable, remains inescapable. The one sure fact of life is that one day, with or without warning, quietly or painfully, it is going to stop. How will I, then, cope with death when my turn comes?

CHRISTIAN VICTORY

Christians hold that the Jesus of the Scriptures is alive and that those who know him as Savior, Lord, and Friend find in this knowledge a way through all life's problems, dying included. For "Christ leads me through no darker rooms / Than he went through before." Having tasted death himself, he can support us while we taste it and carry us through the great change to share the life beyond death into which he himself has passed. Death without Christ is "the king of terrors," but death with Christ loses the "sting," the power to hurt, that it otherwise would have.

John Preston, the Puritan, knew this. When he lay dying, they asked him if he feared death, now that it was so close. "No," whispered Preston; "I shall change my *place*, but I shall not change my *company*." As if to say: I shall leave my friends, but not my Friend, for he will never leave me.

This is victory—victory over death and the fear it brings. And it is to point the way to this victory that the Creed, before announcing Jesus' resurrection, declares: "he descended into hell." Though this clause did not establish itself in the Creed until the fourth century and is therefore not used by some churches, what it says is of very great importance, as we can now see.

HADES, NOT GEHENNA

The English is misleading, for "hell" has changed its sense since the English form of the Creed was fixed. Originally "hell" meant the place of the departed as such, corresponding to the Greek *Hades* and the Hebrew *Sheol*. That is what it means here, where the Creed echoes Peter's statement that

Psalm 16:10, "thou wilt not abandon my soul to *Hades*" (so RSV: AV has "hell"), was a prophecy fulfilled when Jesus rose (see Acts 2:27–31). But since the seventeenth century "hell" has been used to signify only the state of final retribution for the godless, for which the New Testament name is *Gehenna*.

What the Creed means, however, is that Jesus entered, not *Gehenna*, but *Hades*—that is, that he really died, and that it was from a genuine death, not a simulated one, that he rose.

Perhaps it should be said (though one shrinks from laboring something so obvious) that "descended" does *not* imply that the way from Palestine to Hades is down into the ground, any more than "rose" implies that Jesus returned to surface level up the equivalent of a mine shaft! The language of descent is used because Hades, being the place of the disembodied, is *lower* in worth and dignity than is life on earth, where body and soul are together and humanity is in that sense whole.

JESUS IN HADES

"Being put to death in the flesh but made alive in the spirit" (1 Peter 3:18), Jesus entered Hades, and Scripture tells us briefly what he did there.

First, by his presence he made Hades into Paradise (a

place of pleasure) for the penitent thief (cf. Luke 23:43), and presumably for all others who died trusting him during his earthly ministry, just as he does now for the faithful departed (see Philippians 1:21–23; 2 Corinthians 5:6–8).

Second, he perfected the spirits of Old Testament believers (Hebrews 12:23; cf. 11:40), bringing them out of the gloom that Sheol, "the pit," had hitherto been for them (cf. Psalm 88:3–6, 10–12), into this same Paradise experience. This is the core of truth in Medieval fantasies of the "harrowing of hell."

*Now we can face death knowing that when it comes
we shall not find ourselves alone.
He has been there before us,
and he will see us through.*

Third, 1 Peter 3:19 tells us that he "proclaimed" (presumably, about his kingdom and appointment as the world's judge) to the imprisoned "spirits" who had rebelled in antediluvian times (presumably the fallen angels of 2 Peter 2:4ff., who are also "the sons of God" of Genesis 6:1–4). Some have based on this one text a hope that all humans who did not hear the gospel in this life, or who having heard it rejected it, will have it savingly preached to them in the life to come, but Peter's words do not provide the least warrant for that inference.

What makes Jesus' entry into Hades important for us is not, however, any of this, but simply the fact that now we can face death knowing that when it comes we shall not find ourselves alone. He has been there before us, and he will see us through.

FURTHER BIBLE STUDY

The Christian's attitude toward death:
- Philippians 1:19–26
- 2 Corinthians 5:1–10
- 2 Timothy 4:6–18

QUESTIONS FOR THOUGHT AND DISCUSSION

- Define and differentiate the biblical terms *Hades, Sheol, Gehenna.*
- How do we know that Christ's experience of death was genuine? What is the importance of this fact?
- What difference does it make whether we face death with Christ or without him?

And if Christ has not been raised,
your faith is futile and you are still
in your sins.

1 CORINTHIANS 15:17

CHAPTER 11

The Third Day

Suppose that Jesus, having died on the cross, had stayed dead. Suppose that, like Socrates or Confucius, he was now no more than a beautiful memory. Would it matter? We would still have his example and teaching; wouldn't they be enough?

JESUS' RISING IS CRUCIAL

Enough for what? Not for Christianity. Had Jesus not risen but stayed dead, the bottom would drop out of Christianity, for four things would then be true.

First, to quote Paul, in 1 Corinthians 15:17: "if Christ has not been raised, your faith is futile and you are still in your sins."

Second, there is then no hope of our rising either; we must expect to stay dead too.

Third, if Jesus Christ is not risen, then he is not reigning and will not return, and every single item in the Creed after "suffered . . . and [was] buried" would have to be struck out.

Fourth, Christianity cannot be what the first Christians thought it was—fellowship with a living Lord who is identical with the Jesus of the Gospels. The Jesus of the Gospels can still be your hero, but he cannot be your Savior if he did not rise.

A FACT OF HISTORY

To show that it views Jesus' resurrection as a fact of history, the Creed actually times it—"the third day," counting inclusively (the ancients' way) from the day when Jesus "suffered under Pontius Pilate" in about A.D. 30. On that precise day in Jerusalem, the capital of Palestine, Jesus came alive and vacated a rock tomb, and death was conquered for all time.

Can we be sure it happened? The evidence is solid. The tomb was empty, and nobody could produce the body. For more than a month afterward, the disciples kept meeting Jesus alive, always unexpectedly, usually in groups (from two to five hundred). Hallucinations don't happen this way!

The disciples, for their part, were sure that the risen Christ was no fancy and tirelessly proclaimed his rising in the face of ridicule, persecution, and even death—a most effective way of scotching the malicious rumor that they stole Jesus' body (cf. Matthew 28:11–15).

The corporate experience of the Christian church over nineteen centuries chimes in with the belief that Jesus rose, for the risen Lord truly "walks with me and talks with me along life's narrow way," and communion with him belongs to the basic Christian awareness of reality.

No sense can be made of any of this evidence save by supposing that Jesus really rose.

To believe in Jesus Christ as Son of God and living Savior is certainly more than an exercise of reason, but in the face of the evidence it is the only reasonable thing a person can do.

Well might Professor C. F. D. Moule issue his challenge: "If the coming into existence of the Nazarenes, a phenomenon undeniably attested in the New Testament, rips a great hole in history, a hole of the size and shape of the resurrection, what does the secular historian propose to stop it up with?" The actual historical effect is inconceivable without the resurrection of Jesus as its objective historical cause.

FACING THE EVIDENCE

A Christian in public debate accused his skeptical opponent of having more faith than he—"for," he said, "in face of the evidence, I can't believe that Jesus did not rise, and you can!" It really is harder to disbelieve the resurrection than to accept it, much harder. Have you yet seen it that way? To believe in Jesus Christ as Son of God and living Savior, and to echo the words of ex-doubter Thomas, "My Lord and my God," is certainly more than an exercise of reason, but in the face of the evidence it is the only *reasonable* thing a person can do.

WHAT JESUS' RISING MEANS

What is the significance of Jesus' rising? In a word, it marked Jesus out as the Son of God (Romans 1:4); it vindicated his righteousness (John 16:10); it demonstrated victory over death (Acts 2:24); it guaranteed the believer's forgiveness and justification (1 Corinthians 15:17; Romans 4:25) and his own future resurrection too (1 Corinthians 15:18); and it brings him into the reality of resurrection life now (Romans 6:4). Marvelous! You could speak of Jesus' rising as the most hopeful—hope-full—thing that has ever happened—and you would be right!

FURTHER BIBLE STUDY

The resurrection of Jesus:
- John 20:1–18
- 1 Corinthians 15:1–28

QUESTIONS FOR THOUGHT AND DISCUSSION

- How would Christianity be different if Christ had not risen?
- What evidence is there for Jesus' resurrection?
- Why does Packer speak of believing that Christ rose as "the only reasonable thing a person can do"? Do you agree?

Who is to condemn?
Christ Jesus is the one who died—more than that,
who was raised—who is at the right hand of God,
who indeed is interceding for us.

ROMANS 8 : 34

CHAPTER 12

He Ascended into Heaven

"He ascended" echoes Jesus' "I am ascending" (John 20:17; compare 6:62). "Into heaven" echoes "taken up from you into heaven," the angels' words in the Ascension story (Acts 1:11). But what is "heaven"? Is it the sky or outer space? Does the Creed mean that Jesus was the first astronaut? No; both it and the Bible are making a different point.

WHAT HEAVEN MEANS

"Heaven" in the Bible means three things: 1. The endless, self-sustaining life of God. In this sense, God always dwelled in heaven, even when there was no earth. 2. The state of angels or men as they share the life of God, whether in foretaste now or in fullness hereafter. In this sense, the Christian's reward, treasure, and inheritance are all in heaven, and heaven is shorthand for the Christian's final hope. 3. The sky, which, being above us and more like infinity than anything else we know, is an emblem in space and time of God's eternal life, just as the rainbow is an emblem of his everlasting covenant (see Genesis 9:8–17).

The Bible and the Creed proclaim that in the Ascension, forty days after his rising, Jesus entered heaven in sense 2 in a new and momentous way: thenceforth he "sitteth on the right hand of God the Father almighty," ruling all things in his Father's name and with his Father's almightiness for the long-term good of his people. "On the right hand of God" signifies not a palatial location but a regal function: see Acts 2:33ff.; Romans 8:34; Ephesians 1:20ff.; Hebrews 1:3, 13; 10:12ff.; 12:2. He "ascended far above all the heavens" (that is, reentered his pre-incarnate life, a life unrestricted by anything created) "that he might fill all things" (that is, make his kingly power effective everywhere; see Ephesians 4:10). "Ascended" is, of course, a picture-word implying exaltation ("going up!") to a condition of supreme dignity and power.

THE ASCENSION

What happened at the Ascension, then, was not that Jesus became a spaceman, but that his disciples were shown a sign, just as at the Transfiguration. As C. S. Lewis put it, "they saw first a short vertical movement and then a vague luminosity (that is what 'cloud' presumably means . . .) and then nothing." In other words, Jesus' final withdrawal from human sight, to rule until he returns in judgment, was presented to the disciples' outward eyes as a going up into heaven in sense 3. This should not puzzle us. Withdrawal had to take place somehow, and going up, down, or sideways, failing to appear or suddenly vanishing were the only possible ways. Which would signify most clearly that Jesus would henceforth be reigning in glory? That answers itself.

So the message of the Ascension story is: "Jesus the Savior reigns!"

OUR HEARTS IN HEAVEN

In a weary world in which grave philosophers were counseling suicide as man's best option, the unshakable, rollicking optimism of the first Christians, who went on feeling on top of the world however much the world seemed to be on top of them, made a vast impression. (It still does, when Christians are Christian enough to show it!) Three certainties were, and are, its secret.

The first concerns God's *world*. It is that Christ really rules it, that he has won a decisive victory over the dark powers that had mastered it, and that the manifesting of this fact is only a matter of time. God's war with Satan is now like a chess game in which the result is sure but the losing player has not yet given up, or like the last phase of human hostilities in which the defeated enemy's counterattacks, though fierce and frequent, cannot succeed and are embraced in the victor's strategy as mere mopping-up operations. One wishes that our reckoning of dates "A.D." (*anno Domini*, in the year of our Lord), which starts in intention (though probably a few years too late) with Jesus' birth, had been calculated from the year of the cross, resurrection, and ascension, for that was when Jesus' Lordship became the cosmic fact that it is today.

In a weary world in which grave philosophers were counseling suicide as man's best option, the unshakable, rollicking optimism of the first Christians, who went on feeling on top of the world however much the world seemed to be on top of them, made a vast impression. (It still does, when Christians are Christian enough to show it!)

The second certainty concerns God's *Christ*. It is that our reigning Lord is "interceding" for us (Romans 8:34; Hebrews 7:25), in the sense that he appears "in the presence of God" as our "advocate" (Hebrews 9:24; 1 John 2:1) to ensure that we receive "grace to help" in our need (Hebrews 4:16) and so are kept to the end in the love of God (cf. the Good Shepherd's pledge, John 10:27–29). "Interceding" denotes not a suppliant making an appeal to charity, but the intervening of one who has sovereign right and power to make requests and take action in another's interest. It is truly said that our Lord's presence and life in heaven as the enthroned priest-king, our propitiation, so to speak, in person, is itself his intercession: just for him to be there guarantees all grace to us, and glory too.

An eighteenth-century jingle puts this certainty into words that make the heart leap:

Love moved thee to die;
And on this I rely,
My Saviour hath loved me, I cannot tell why:
But this I can find,
We two are so joined
He'll not be in glory and leave me behind.

The third certainty concerns God's people. It is a matter of God-given experience as well as of God-taught understanding. It is that Christians enjoy here and now a hidden life of fellowship with the Father and the Son that nothing, not even death itself, can touch—for it is the life of the world to come begun already, the life of heaven tasted here on earth. The explanation of this experience, which all God's people know in some measure, is that believers have actually passed through death (not as a physical but as a personal and psychic event) into the eternal life that lies beyond. "You have died, and your life is hidden with Christ in God" (Colossians 3:3; cf. 2:12; Romans 6:3–4). "God . . . when we were dead . . . made us alive together with Christ . . . and raised us up with him and seated us with him in the heavenly places in Christ Jesus" (Ephesians 2:4ff.).

The prayer used on Ascension Day in the Anglican Prayer Book asks God to "grant . . . that like as we do believe thy only-begotten Son our Lord Jesus Christ to have ascended into heavens; so we may also in heart and mind thither ascend, and with him continually dwell." May we be enabled, in the power of these three certainties, to do just that.

FURTHER BIBLE STUDY

The significance of the Ascension:
- Acts 1:1–11
- Ephesians 1:15–2:10

QUESTIONS FOR THOUGHT AND DISCUSSION

- In what sense did Jesus ascend to heaven?
- To what did he return?
- What is Christ doing now? What importance has this heavenly ministry for us?

*"You also must be ready,
for the Son of Man is coming
at an hour you do not expect."*

MATTHEW 24:44

CHAPTER 13

He Shall Come

The core of the Creed is its witness to the past, present, and future of Jesus Christ: his birth, death, rising, and ascension in the past; his reign now; and his coming at a future date to judge. ("Quick" in "the quick and the dead," by the way, means living, not fast-moving.) With his coming, Scripture tells us, will come our bodily resurrection and the full everlasting life of which the Creed speaks. A new cosmic order will start then too. There's a great day coming. (See Matthew 25:14–46; John 5:25–29; Romans 8:18–24; 2 Peter 3:10–13; Revelation 20:11–21:4.)

THE CHRISTIAN'S HOPE

Nowhere does the strength of the Creed as a charter for life come out more clearly. In today's world, pessimism prevails because people lack hope. They foresee only the bomb or bankruptcy or a weary old age—nothing worthwhile. Communists and Jehovah's Witnesses attract by offering bright hopes of heaven on earth—following the Revolution in one case, Armageddon in the other. But Christians have a hope that outshines both—the hope of which Bunyan's Mr. Stand-fast said, "The thoughts of what I am going to . . . lie as a glowing Coal at my Heart." The Creed highlights this hope when it declares: "he shall come."

In one sense, Christ comes for every Christian at death, but the Creed looks to the day when he will come publicly to wind up history and judge all men—Christians as Christians, accepted already, whom a "blood-bought free reward" [from the hymn, "There Is a Fountain Filled with Blood"] awaits according to the faithfulness of their service; rebels as rebels, to be rejected by the Master whom they rejected first. The judgments of Jesus, "the righteous judge" (2 Timothy 4:8; compare Romans 2:5–11), will raise no moral problems.

CERTAIN AND GLORIOUS

Some think this will never happen, but we have God's word for it, and sober scientists now tell us that an end to our world through nuclear or ecological catastrophe is a real possibility. Christ's coming is unimaginable—but man's imagination is no measure of God's power, and the Jesus who is spiritually present to millions simultaneously now can surely make himself visibly present to the risen race then. We do not know when he will come (so we must always be ready), nor how he will come (why not in the going off of a bomb?). But "we know that when he appears we shall be like him, because we shall see him as he is" (1 John 3:2)—and that is knowledge enough! "Come, Lord Jesus!" (Revelation 22:20).

ECLIPSED

The hope of Christ's return thrilled the New Testament Christians, as witness over three hundred references to it in the documents—on average, one every thirteen verses. But to us it is not so much exciting as embarrassing! The phrase "Cinderella of the Creed," which was once applied to the Holy Spirit, nowadays fits Christ's return much more truly. Why is it thus in eclipse? For four main reasons, it seems.

First, this is a time of *reaction* from a century and a half of intense prophetic study expressing a spirit of prayerless pessimism about the church and doom-watching detachment from the world. This spirit, and the dogmatism that went with it about both the signs and the date of Christ's coming (despite Mark 13:32 and Acts 1:7!), were quite unjustifiable and have given the topic a bad name.

Second, this is a time of *skepticism* as to whether Christ

personally and physically rose and ascended, and this naturally spawns dithering doubts as to whether we can hope ever to see him again.

We think less and less about the better things that Christ will bring us at his reappearance because our thoughts are increasingly absorbed by the good things we enjoy here.

Third, this is a time of *timidity*, in which Christians, while querying the materialistic self-sufficiency of Western secularism and Marxist ideologies, hesitate to challenge their "this-worldly" preoccupation, lest the counter-accusation be provoked that Christians do not care about social and economic justice. So the fact that Christ will end this world, and that the best part of the Christian hope lies beyond it, gets played down.

Fourth, this is a time of *worldly-mindedness*, at least among the prosperous Christians of the West. We think less and less about the better things that Christ will bring us at his reappearance because our thoughts are increasingly absorbed by the good things we enjoy here. No one would wish persecution or destitution on another, but who can deny that at this point they might do us good?

All four attitudes are unhealthy and unworthy. God help us to transcend them.

BE PREPARED

"Be ready," said the Savior to his disciples, "for the Son of man is coming at an hour you do not expect" (Matthew 24:44). How does one get and stay ready? By keeping short accounts with God and men; by taking life a day at a time, as Jesus told us to do (Matthew 6:34); and by heeding the advice of Bishop Ken's hymn, "Live each day as if thy last." Budget and plan for an ordinary span of years, but in spirit be packed up and ready to leave at any time. This should be part of our daily devotional discipline. When the Lord comes, he should find his people praying for revival and planning world evangelism—but packed up and ready to leave nonetheless. If Boy Scouts can learn to live realistically in terms of the motto "Be prepared" for any ordinary thing that might happen, why are Christians so slow to learn the same lesson in relation to the momentous event of Christ's return?

FURTHER BIBLE STUDY

The Christian's attitude toward Christ's return:

- Luke 12:35–48
- 1 Thessalonians 4:13–5:11
- 2 Peter 3

QUESTIONS FOR THOUGHT AND DISCUSSION

- In what way is Christ's future coming reason for hope?
- When Christ returns, what will he do? What are your reactions to knowing this?
- What does the Bible not tell us about Christ's return? Why do you think God withholds this information?

*"And I will ask the Father, and he will give you
another Helper, to be with you forever,
even the Spirit of truth, whom the world
cannot receive, because it neither sees him
nor knows him. You know him, for he dwells
with you and will be in you."*

JOHN 14:16–17

CHAPTER 14

I Believe in the Holy Spirit

I believe in the Holy Spirit": so starts the Creed's third paragraph. From the creating work of the Father and the rescue work of the Son, it turns to the re-creating work of the Spirit, whereby we are actually made new in and through Christ. So we hear of *church* (new community), *forgiveness* (new relationship), *resurrection* (new existence), and *everlasting life* (new fulfillment). But first comes a profession of faith in the Spirit himself.

THE SPIRIT OF CHRIST

He is divine ("Holy," says this). He is an active Person, the Executive of the Godhead. Yes, but doing and aiming at what? Misbelief abounds here. Some associate the Spirit with mystical states and artistic inspirations, both Christian and pagan. Others link the Spirit only with unusual Christian experiences—feeling "high" (to use the world's word), seeking visions, receiving revelations, speaking in tongues, healing. But these are secondary elements of the Spirit's work, where they derive from the Spirit at all.

The Old Testament mentions the Spirit in connection with creation, both divine (Genesis 1:2) and human (Exodus 31:1–6); the inspiring of God's spokesmen (Isaiah 61:1; the Nicene Creed states that the Spirit "spoke by the prophets"); the equipping and enabling of God's servants (judges, kings, etc.; e.g., Judges 13:25; 14:19; Isaiah 11:2; Zechariah 4:6); and the evoking of godliness in individuals and in the community (Psalm 51:11; Ezekiel 36:26ff.; 37:1–14; Zechariah 12:10). All this gains deeper meaning in the New Testament, where the Spirit is shown to be a personal agent distinct from the Father and the Son and is spoken of as "the Spirit of Christ" (Romans 8:9; 1 Peter 1:11).

The Spirit shows Jesus to us through the gospel, unites us to him by faith, and indwells us to change us "into [his] image" by causing "the fruit of the Spirit" to grow in us.

The key to understanding the New Testament view of the Spirit's work is to see that his purpose is identical with the

Father's—namely, to see glory and praise come to the Son. Accordingly—

First, the Spirit serviced the Son throughout his earthly life from the moment when, as the Creed says, he was "conceived by the Holy Spirit" (Matthew 1:20). The Spirit's dovelike descent on him at his baptism showed not only that Jesus was the Spirit-giver, but also that he was himself Spirit-filled (Luke 4:1; cf. verses 14, 18). It was "through the eternal Spirit" that he offered himself in sacrifice for us (Hebrews 9:14).

Second, the Spirit now acts as Jesus' agent—"another Helper" (John 14:16; helper, supporter, advocate, encourager). He shows Jesus to us through the gospel, unites us to him by faith, and indwells us to change us "into [his] image" by causing "the fruit of the Spirit" to grow in us (2 Corinthians 3:18; Galatians 5:22ff.).

"He will glorify [not himself but] me, for he will take what is mine and declare it to you" (John 16:14). Jesus' words indicate the self-effacing character of the Spirit; he functions as a floodlight trained on Christ, so that it is Christ, not the Spirit, whom we see. In the gospel message, Jesus is set before us throughout, saying: "Come to me; follow me." In our conscience as we hear the gospel with the inner ear of faith, the Spirit, standing behind us as it were to throw light over our shoulder onto Jesus, constantly urges, "Go to him; deal with him." So we do—and it is this that makes our life Christian.

WITNESS AND MINISTRY

The Spirit is *witness* and *teacher* (1 John 5:7; 2:27; cf. 4:2ff.) inasmuch as, first, he convinces us that the Jesus of the gospel, the New Testament Christ, really exists and is what he is "for us men, and for our salvation" [Nicene Creed]; second, he assures us that as believers we are God's children and heirs with Christ (Romans 8:16ff.); third, he moves us to bear witness to the Christ whom his witness led us to know (cf. John 15:26). What the Spirit's witnessing effects is not private revelation of something hitherto undisclosed but personal reception of God's public testimony that was there all along in the Scriptures but went unheeded. Paul is describing the Spirit's work of witness when he speaks of "having the eyes of your hearts enlightened" (Ephesians 1:18).

Third, the Spirit gives to every Christian one or more gifts (i.e., capacities to express Christ in serving God and man), so that every-member ministry in the church, which is Christ's body, may become a reality (1 Corinthians 12:4–7; Ephesians 4:11–16). This manifold ministry is itself Christ's own ministry continuing from heaven, through us as his hands, feet, and mouth; and the Spirit's bestowing of gifts should be seen as further servicing and glorifying Christ on his part, inasmuch as it is the means whereby Christ's personal ministry to men is able to go on.

SIGNS OF THE SPIRIT

What then are the signs that Christ's self-effacing Spirit is at work? Not mystical raptures, nor visions and supposed revelations, nor even healings, tongues, and apparent miracles; for Satan, playing on our psychosomatic complexity and our fallenness, can produce all these things (cf. 2 Thessalonians 2:9ff.; Colossians 2:18). The only sure signs are that the Christ of the Bible is acknowledged, trusted, loved for his grace, and served for his glory and that believers actually turn from sin to the life of holiness that is Christ's image in his people (cf. 1 Corinthians 12:3; 2 Corinthians 3:17). These are the criteria by which we must judge, for instance, the modern "charismatic renewal" and Christian Science (reaching, perhaps, different verdicts in the two cases).

So when I say, as a Christian, "I believe in the Holy Spirit," my meaning should be, first, that I believe personal fellowship, across space and time, with the living Christ of the New Testament to be a reality, which through the Spirit I have found; second, that I am open to being led by the Spirit, who now indwells me, into Christian knowledge, obedience, and service, and I expect to be so led each day; and, third, that I bless him as the author of my assurance that I am a son and heir of God. Truly, it is a glorious thing to believe in the Holy Spirit!

FURTHER BIBLE STUDY

The Spirit's ministry:
- John 7:37–39; 14:15–26; 16:7–15
- Romans 8:1–17

QUESTIONS FOR THOUGHT AND DISCUSSION

- How does the work of the Spirit differ from that of the Father and the Son?
- What does the Holy Spirit do as "Jesus' agent"?
- What would you say to a professed Christian who doubted if he had ever experienced the ministry of the Holy Spirit?

*You yourselves like living stones are being
built up as a spiritual house, to be a
holy priesthood, to offer spiritual sacrifices
acceptable to God through Jesus Christ . . . you
are a chosen race, a royal priesthood,
a holy nation, a people for his own possession,
that you may proclaim the excellencies of
him who called you out of darkness
into his marvelous light.*

1 PETER 2:5, 9

CHAPTER 15

The Holy Catholic Church

It is by strict theological logic that the Creed confesses faith in the Holy Spirit before proceeding to the church and that it speaks of the church before mentioning personal salvation (forgiveness, resurrection, everlasting life). For though Father and Son have loved the church and the Son has redeemed it, it is the Holy Spirit who actually creates it, by inducing faith; and it is in the church, through its ministry and fellowship, that personal salvation ordinarily comes to be enjoyed.

Unhappily, there is at this point a parting of the ways. Roman Catholics and Protestants both say the Creed, yet they are divided. Why? Basically, because of divergent understandings of "I believe in the holy catholic church"—"one holy catholic and apostolic church," as the true text of the Nicene Creed has it.

ROMAN VERSUS PROTESTANT

Official Roman Catholic teaching presents the church of Christ as the *one* organized body of baptized persons who are in communion with the Pope and acknowledge the teaching and ruling authority of the episcopal hierarchy. It is *holy* because it produces saintly folk and is kept from radical sin, *catholic* because in its worldwide spread it holds the full faith in trust for everyone, and *apostolic* because its ministerial orders stem from the apostles, and its faith (including such non-biblical items as the assumption of Mary and her immaculate conception, the Mass-sacrifice, and papal infallibility) is a sound growth from apostolic roots. Non-Roman bodies, however church-like, are not strictly part of the church at all.

Protestants challenge this from the Bible. In Scripture (they say) the church is the *one* worldwide fellowship of believing people whose Head is Christ. It is *holy* because it is consecrated to God (though it is capable nonetheless of grievous sin); it is *catholic* because it embraces all Christians everywhere; and it is *apostolic* because it seeks to maintain the apostles' doctrine unmixed. Pope, hierarchy, and extra-biblical doctrines are not merely nonessential but actually deforming; if Rome is a church (which some Reformers doubted) she is so despite the extras, not because of them. In particular, infallibility belongs to God speaking in the Bible, not to the church or to any of its officers, and any teaching given in or by the church must be open to correction by "God's word written."[1]

Some Protestants have taken the clause "the communion of saints," which follows "the holy catholic church," as the Creed's own elucidation of what the church is; namely, Christians in fellowship with each other—just that, without regard for any particular hierarchical structure. But it is usual to treat this phrase as affirming the real union in Christ of the church "militant here on earth" with the church triumphant, as is indicated in Hebrews 12:22–24; and it may be that the clause was originally meant to signify *communion in holy things* (Word, sacrament, worship, prayers) and to make the true but distinct point that in the church there is a real sharing in the life of God. The "spiritual" view of the church as being a fellowship before it is an institution can, however, be confirmed from Scripture without appeal to this phrase, whatever its sense, being needed.

THE NEW TESTAMENT

That the New Testament presents the Protestant view is hardly open to dispute (the dispute is over whether the New Testament is final!). The church appears in Trinitarian relationships as the family of God the Father, the body of Christ the Son, and the temple (dwelling-place) of the Holy Spirit, and so long as the dominical sacraments are administered and ministerial oversight is exercised, no organizational norms are insisted on at all. The church is the supernatural society of God's redeemed and baptized people, looking back to Christ's first coming with gratitude and on to his second coming with hope. "Your life is hidden with Christ in God. When Christ who is your life appears, then you also will appear with him in glory" (Colossians 3:3–4)—such is the church's present state and future prospect. To this hope both sacraments point, baptism prefiguring final resurrection, the Lord's Supper anticipating "the marriage supper of the Lamb" (Revelation 19:9).

The church is the supernatural society of God's redeemed and baptized people, looking back to Christ's first coming with gratitude and on to his second coming with hope.

For the present, however, all churches (like those in Corinth, Colosse, Galatia, and Thessalonica, to look no further) are prone to err in both faith and morals and need constant correction and re-formation at all levels (intellectual, devotional, structural, liturgical) by the Spirit through God's Word.

The evangelical theology of revival, first spelled out in the seventeenth and eighteenth centuries, and the present-day emergence of "charismatic renewal" on a worldwide scale remind us of something that Roman Catholic and Protestant disputers, in their concentration on doctrinal truth, tended to miss—namely, that the church must always be open to the immediacy of the Spirit's Lordship and that disorderly vigor in a congregation is infinitely preferable to a correct and tidy deadness.

THE LOCAL CHURCH

The acid test of the church's state is what happens in the local congregation. Each congregation is a visible outcrop of the one church universal, called to serve God and men in humility and, perhaps, humiliation while living in prospect of glory. Spirit-filled for worship and witness, active in love and care for insiders and outsiders alike, self-supporting and self-propagating, each congregation is to be a spearhead of divine counterattack for the recapture of a rebel world.

Here is a question for you: how is your congregation getting on?

FURTHER BIBLE STUDY

The church's nature and destiny:
- 1 Peter 2
- Ephesians 2:11–4:16

QUESTIONS FOR THOUGHT AND DISCUSSION

- How does the Roman Catholic use of the New Testament differ from the Protestant one? How does this affect the concept each holds of the church?
- How does Packer define "the communion of saints"? Do you agree with what he says? Why or why not?
- What is the function of a local Christian church in relation to the universal church?

NOTE

[1]Anglican Article XX.

If you, O LORD, should mark iniquities,
O Lord, who could stand?
But with you there is forgiveness,
that you may be feared.

PSALM 130:3–4

CHAPTER 16

Forgiveness of Sins

What are *sins*? Sin, says the Westminster Shorter Catechism, is "any want of conformity unto, or transgression of, the law of God." This echoes 1 John 3:4, "sin is lawlessness." It has other aspects too. It is lawlessness in relation to God as lawgiver, rebellion in relation to God as rightful ruler, missing the mark in relation to God as our designer, guilt in relation to God as judge, and uncleanness in relation to God as the Holy One.

Sin is a perversity touching each one of us at every point in our lives. Apart from Jesus Christ, no human being has ever been free of its infection. It appears in desires as well as deeds, and in motives as well as actions. The Anglican Prayer Book rightly teaches that "We have followed too much the devices and desires of our own hearts. . . . We have left undone those things which we ought to have done, and we have done those things which we ought not to have done, and (spiritually) there is no health in us."

Sin is everybody's problem in the sight of God, for he is "of purer eyes than to see evil" and "cannot look at wrong" (Habakkuk 1:13). But we find life to be a moral minefield for us; and the harder we try to avoid sin, the more often we find—too late—that we have stepped where we shouldn't and have been blown to pieces so far as the required love of God and our neighbor is concerned. And where does that leave us?—"the wrath of God is revealed from heaven against all ungodliness and unrighteousness of men" (Romans 1:18).

The good news, however, is this—sins can be forgiven. Central to the gospel is the glorious "but" of Psalm 130:4—"If you, O LORD, should mark iniquities, O Lord, who could stand? *But* with you there is forgiveness, that you may be feared"—that is, worshiped with loyalty (for that is what *fear* of God means).

VITAL AND REAL

Forgiveness is pardon in a personal setting. It is taking back into friendship those who went against you, hurt you, and put themselves in the wrong with you. It is *compassionate* (showing unmerited kindness to the wrongdoer), *creative* (renewing the spoiled relationship), and, inevitably, *costly*.

God's forgiveness is the supreme instance of this, for it is God in love restoring fellowship at the cost of the cross.

Forgiveness is taking back into friendship those who went against you, hurt you, and put themselves in the wrong with you. God's forgiveness is the supreme instance of this, for it is God in love restoring fellowship at the cost of the cross.

If our sins were unforgivable, where would we be? A bad conscience is the most universal experience—and the most wretched. No outward change relieves it; you carry it with you all your waking hours. The more conscientious you are, the more your knowledge of having failed others, and God, too, will haunt you. Without forgiveness you will have no peace. A bad conscience delivering at full strength, tearing you to pieces in the name of God, is hell indeed, both here and hereafter.

LUTHER KNEW IT

A man distressed about sin wrote to Luther. The Reformer, who himself had suffered long agonies over this problem, replied: "Learn to know Christ and him crucified. Learn to sing to him and say—Lord Jesus, you are my righteousness, I am your sin. You took on you what was mine; you set on me what was yours. You became what you were not that I might become what I was not." Compare Paul: "For our sake [God] made [Christ] to be sin who knew no sin, so that in him we might become the righteousness of God" (2 Corinthians 5:21). Link up with Jesus, the living Lord, by faith, and the great exchange is fulfilled. Through Jesus' atoning death God accepts you as righteous and cancels your sins. This is justification, forgiveness, and peace.

Paul in Romans and Galatians, and the Reformers after him, spoke of justification rather than of forgiveness. This is because justification is forgiveness *plus*; it signifies not only a washing out of the past but also acceptance and the gift of a righteous man's status for the future. Also, justification is final, being a decision on which God will never go back, and so it is the basis of assurance, whereas present forgiveness does not necessarily argue more than temporary forbearance. So justification—public acquittal and reinstatement before God's judgment-seat—is actually the richer concept.

BY FAITH ONLY

In the past (things are less clear-cut today) Roman Catholics did not grasp the decisiveness of present justification, nor see that Christ's righteousness ("my Savior's obedience and blood," as Toplady put it) is its whole ground, nor realize that our part is to stop trying to earn it and to simply take it as God's free gift of grace. So they insisted that sacraments, "good works," and purgatorial pains hereafter were all necessary means of final acceptance, because they were among the grounds on which that acceptance was based. But the Reformers preached, as Paul did, full and final acceptance through a decisive act of forgiveness here and now; and this, they said, is by faith only.

Why faith *only*? Because Christ's righteousness *only* is the basis of pardon and peace, and Christ and his gifts are received *only* by faith's embrace. Faith means not only believing God's truth but trusting Christ, taking what he offers, and then triumphing in the knowledge of what is now yours.

Is God's gift of forgiveness by faith yours yet? It is easily missed. The Jews missed it, said Paul; their tragedy was that their "zeal for God" led them to try to establish their own righteousness (i.e., to earn his acceptance), and "they did not submit to God's righteousness" (i.e., to his way of forgiving and justifying, by faith in Christ only): see Romans 10:2ff. The pathetic truth is that we sinners are self-righteous to the core, and we are constantly justifying ourselves, and we hate admitting that there is anything seriously wrong with us, anything that God or man might seriously hold against us; and we have to do violence to our own perverted instincts at this point before faith is possible for us. God save us all from repeating the tragedy of the Jews in our own lives.

FURTHER BIBLE STUDY

Justification through Christ by faith apart from works:
- Romans 5; 10:1–13
- Galatians 2:15—3:29
- Philippians 3:4–16

QUESTIONS FOR THOUGHT AND DISCUSSION

- What is forgiveness, and what does it do for the forgiven on a personal level?
- What did Luther mean by saying, "You became what you were not that I might become what I was not"?
- Why is it that forgiveness comes through faith only?

But our citizenship is in heaven,
and from it we await a Savior,
the Lord Jesus Christ, who will transform
our lowly body to be like his glorious body,
by the power that enables him even to
subject all things to himself.

PHILIPPIANS 3:20–21

Resurrection of the Body

Scripture sees death—life's one certainty—not as a friend but as a destroyer. When my body and soul separate, I shall only be a shadow of what I was. My body is part of me, the apparatus of my self-expression; without it, all my power to make things, do things, and relate to my fellows is gone. Think of someone with full use of his faculties, and compare him with a paralytic; now compare the paralytic with someone totally disembodied, and you will see what I mean. Paralytics can do little enough; disembodied persons, less still. Thus death, while not ending our existence, nullifies and in a real sense destroys it.

COPING WITH DEATH

Death is the fundamental human problem, for if death is really final, then nothing is worthwhile save self-indulgence.

"If the dead are not raised, let us eat and drink, for tomorrow we die" (1 Corinthians 15:32). And no philosophy or religion that cannot come to terms with death is any real use to us.

Here, however, Christianity stands out. Alone among the world's faiths and "isms" it views death as conquered. For Christian faith is hope resting on fact—namely, the fact that Jesus rose bodily from the grave and now lives eternally in heaven. The hope is that when Jesus comes back—the day when history stops and this world ends—he will "transform our lowly body to be like his glorious body" (Philippians 3:21; cf. 1 John 3:2). This hope embraces all who have died in Christ as well as Christians alive at his appearing: "for an hour is coming when all who are in the tombs will hear [Jesus'] voice and come out, those who have done good to the resurrection of life" (John 5:28ff.). And the raising of the *body* means the restoring of the *person*—not just part of me, but all of me—to active, creative, undying life, for God and with God.

NEW BODY

In raising believers, God completes their redemption by the gift not of their old bodies somehow patched up, but of new bodies fit for new men. Through regeneration and sanctification God has already renewed us inwardly; now we receive bodies to match. The new body is linked with the old, yet is different from it, just as plants are linked with, yet different from, the seeds from which they grew (see 1 Corinthians 15:35–44). My present body—"brother ass," as Francis of Assisi would have me call it—is like a student's old jalopy; care for it as I will, it goes precariously and never very well and often lets me and my Master down (very frustrating!). But my new body will feel and behave like a Rolls-Royce, and then my service will no longer be spoiled.

In raising believers, God completes their redemption by the gift not of their old bodies somehow patched up, but of new bodies fit for new men.

No doubt, like me, you both love your body because it is part of you and get mad at the way it limits you. So we should. And it is good to know that God's aim in giving us second-rate physical frames here is to prepare us for managing better bodies hereafter. As C. S. Lewis says somewhere, they give you unimpressive horses to learn to ride on, and only when you are ready for it are you allowed an animal that will gallop and jump.

A dwarf I knew would weep for joy at the thought of the body God has in store for him on resurrection day, and when

I think of other Christians known to me who in one way or another are physical wrecks—deformed, decaying, crippled, hormonally unbalanced, or otherwise handicapped—I can weep too for this particular element of joy that will be theirs—and yours and mine—when that day dawns.

Soul and Body

This bit of the Creed was probably put in to ward off the idea (very common for three centuries after Christ, and not unknown today) that man's hope is immortality for his soul, which (so it was thought) would be much better off disembodied. There was a tag, "the body is a tomb," that summed up this view. But it shows a wrong view both of matter (which God made and likes and declares good) and of man (who is not a noble soul able to excuse the shameful things he does by blaming them on his uncouth material shell, but a psycho-physical unit whose moral state is directly expressed by his physical behavior). The disordering effect of sin is very clear in the way my physical appetites function (not to look further); but for all that these appetites are part of me and I must acknowledge moral responsibility for whatever active expression they find. The Bible doctrine of judgment is that each of us will "receive what is due for what he has done in the body, whether good or evil" (2 Corinthians 5:10).

LIKE CHRIST

The promise that one day we will have bodies "like his glorious body" (Philippians 3:20ff.) challenges us—do we really, from our hearts, welcome and embrace our promised destiny of being like Christ? (Cf. 1 John 3:2ff.) Facing this question could be a moment of truth for us. Some find their whole identity in gratifying physical itches (for sexual excitement, sleep, food, exercise, violence, alcoholic or drug-induced "highs," or whatever) and feel—alas, with too much truth— that were they deprived of these, nothing would be left of them but an ache. And they see Jesus, who was not led by physical itches, as the "pale Galilean" through whose breath, according to Swinburne, the world grew cold, and whom D. H. Lawrence wanted to humanize (I have to use that verb in fairness to Lawrence, though it is the wackiest nonsense I have ever written) by imagining for him a sex life with a pagan priestess. Such a vision makes the idea of being like Jesus—that and no more—sound like being sentenced to a living death. Now is that how, deep down, it sounds to you?

If so, only one thing can be said. Ask God to show you how Jesus' life, body and soul, was the only fully human life that has ever been lived, and keep looking at Jesus as you meet him in the Gospels until you can see it. Then the prospect of being like him—that and no less—will seem to you the noblest and most magnificent destiny possible, and by embracing it you will become a true disciple. But until you see it—please believe me: I kid you not—there is no hope for you at all.

FURTHER BIBLE STUDY

The resurrection hope:
- Mark 12:18–27
- 1 Corinthians 15:35–58
- Philippians 3:4–16

QUESTIONS FOR THOUGHT AND DISCUSSION

- Why is a religion that does not deal with death valueless to us?
- What evidence does the Bible give to show that death has been conquered?
- How much can we say that we know about the state of the resurrected?

Then I saw a new heaven and a new earth. . . .
And I heard a loud voice from the throne
saying, "Behold, the dwelling place of God is
with man. He will dwell with them,
and they will be his people, and God himself
will be with them as their God" . . .
the Lord God will be their light,
and they will reign forever and ever.

REVELATION 21:1, 3; 22:5

CHAPTER 18

The Life Everlasting

Skeptics like Fred Hoyle and Bertrand Russell have told us that the thought of an endless future life horrifies them; for (they said) it would be so boring! Evidently they have found this life boring and cannot imagine how human existence could be made permanently interesting and worthwhile. Poor fellows! Here we see the blighting effects of godlessness and the black pessimism to which it leads.

But not all moderns are like Hoyle and Russell. Some are anxious to survive death. Hence their interest in spiritist phenomena, supposed to give proof of survival. But three facts should be noted. First, "messages" from the departed are distressingly trivial and self-absorbed. Second, "messages" do not come from those who in this life walked close to God. Third, mediums and their "controls" are embarrassed by the name of Jesus. These facts give warning that the spiritist phenomena, whatever their true explanation, are a blind alley for investigating "the blessed hope of everlasting life" [*The Book of Common Prayer*].

JESUS' PRESENCE MAKES HEAVEN

When the Creed speaks of "*the* life everlasting," it means not just endless existence (demons and lost souls have that), but the final joy into which Jesus entered (Hebrews 12:2) and which he promised and prayed that his followers would one day share. "Where I am, there will my servant be also. If anyone serves me, the Father will honor him." "Father, I desire that they also, whom you have given me, may be with me where I am, to see my glory" (John 12:26; 17:24).

Being with Jesus is the essence of heaven; it is what the life everlasting is all about.

Being with Jesus is the essence of heaven; it is what the life everlasting is all about. "I have formerly lived by hearsay and faith," said Bunyan's Mr. Stand-fast, "but now I go where I shall live by sight, and shall be with him, in whose company I delight myself." What will we do in heaven? Not lounge around, but worship, work, think and communicate, enjoying activity, beauty, people, and God. First and foremost, however, we shall see and love Jesus, our Savior, Master, and Friend.

ENDLESS JOY

The everlastingness of this life was spelled out in the most vivid possible way by the anonymous benefactor who appended to John Newton's "Amazing Grace" this extra verse:

When we've been there ten thousand years,
Bright shining as the sun,
We've no less days to sing God's praise
Than when we first begun.

I have been writing with enthusiasm, for this everlasting life is something to which I look forward. Why? Not because I am out of love with life here—just the reverse! My life is full of joy, from four sources—knowing God and people and the good and pleasant things that God and men under God have created and doing things that are worthwhile for God or others or for myself as God's man. But my reach exceeds my grasp. My relationships with God and others are never as rich and full as I want them to be, and I am always finding more than I thought was there in great music, great verse, great books, great lives, and the great kaleidoscope of the natural order.

As I get older, I find that I appreciate God and people and good and lovely and noble things more and more intensely; so it is pure delight to think that this enjoyment will continue and increase in some form (what form, God knows, and I am content to wait and see) literally forever. Christians inherit in fact the destiny that fairy tales envisage in fancy: *we* (yes, you and I, the silly, saved sinners) *live*, and live *happily*, and by God's endless mercy will live happily *ever after*.

We cannot visualize heaven's life, and the wise man will not try. Instead he will dwell on the doctrine of heaven, which is that there the redeemed find all their heart's desire—joy with their Lord, joy with his people, and joy in the ending of all frustration and distress and the supply of all wants. What was said to the child—"If you want sweets and hamsters in heaven, they'll be there"—was not an evasion, but a witness to the truth that in heaven no felt needs or longings go unsatisfied. What our wants will actually be, however, we hardly know, save that first and foremost we shall want to "always be with the Lord" (1 Thessalonians 4:17).

Often now we say in moments of great enjoyment, "I don't want this ever to stop," but it does. Heaven, however, is different. May heaven's joys be yours and mine.

FURTHER BIBLE STUDY

Our destination:
• Revelation 21:1–22:5

QUESTIONS FOR THOUGHT AND DISCUSSION

- Why is Packer suspicious of spiritist phenomena?
- Why will heaven be delightful? Do you personally expect and look forward to heaven? Why or why not?
- What will the residents of heaven do?

Scripture Index

Personal Reflections

Personal Reflections

Personal Reflections

Personal Reflections

Personal Reflections